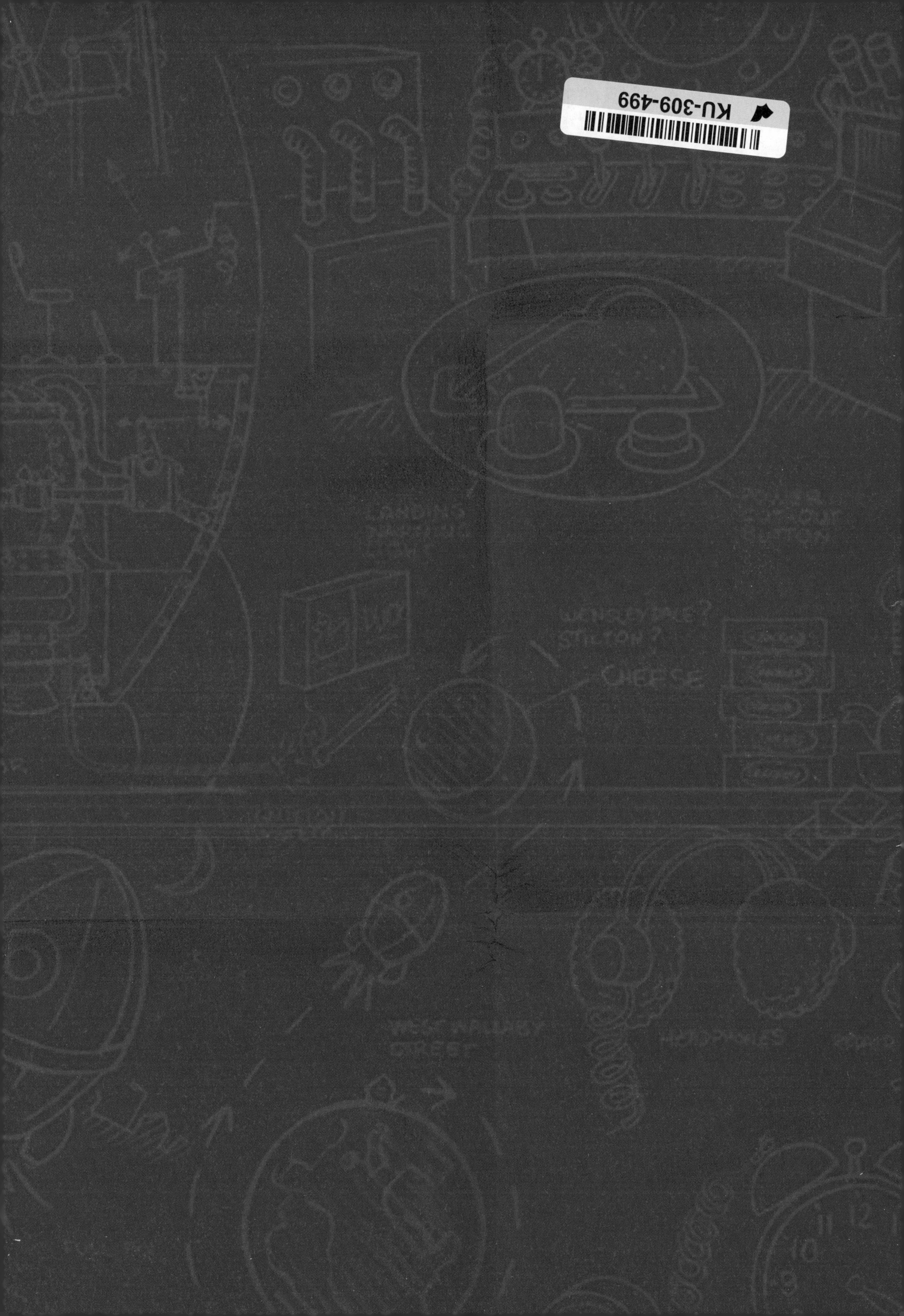
LANDING
WENSLEYDALE ?
STILTON ?
CHEESE

Aardman
presents

Wallace & Gromit ™

Plots In Space

Titan Books

HB ISBN 1 84576 362 9
HB ISBN-13 9781845763626

PB ISBN 1 84576 642 3
PB ISBN-13 9781845766429

Published by Titan Books,
a division of Titan Publishing Group Ltd.
144 Southwark Street
London SE1 0UP
In association with Aardman Animation Ltd.

Grateful thanks and salutations to Dick Hansom and Jess Houston at
Aardman Animations, and David Barraclough, Karl.Barr, Bob Kelly,
Emily Norris, Jamie Boardman and Katy Wild at Titan Books.

A CIP catalogue record for this title is available at the British Library.

First Published May 2007

1 3 5 7 9 10 8 6 4 2

Printed in Italy.

What did you think of this book? We love to hear from our readers. Please email us at:
readerfeedback@titanemail.com, or write to us at the above address.

To subscribe to our regular newsletter for up-to-the-minute news, great offers and
competitions, email: booksezine@titanemail.com with "subscribe" in the subject header.

www.titankids.com/wallaceandgromit
www.wallaceandgromit.com

★ **Aardman**
presents

Wallace & Gromit ™
Plots In Space

Original story by Nick Jones and Steve White

Written by Dan Abnett

Drawn by Jimmy Hansen

Inks by Bambos Georgiou

Coloured by Andrew James

Lettered by Richard Starkings

Edited by Nick Jones and Steve White

Wallace and Gromit created by Nick Park

WALLACE'S GUIDE

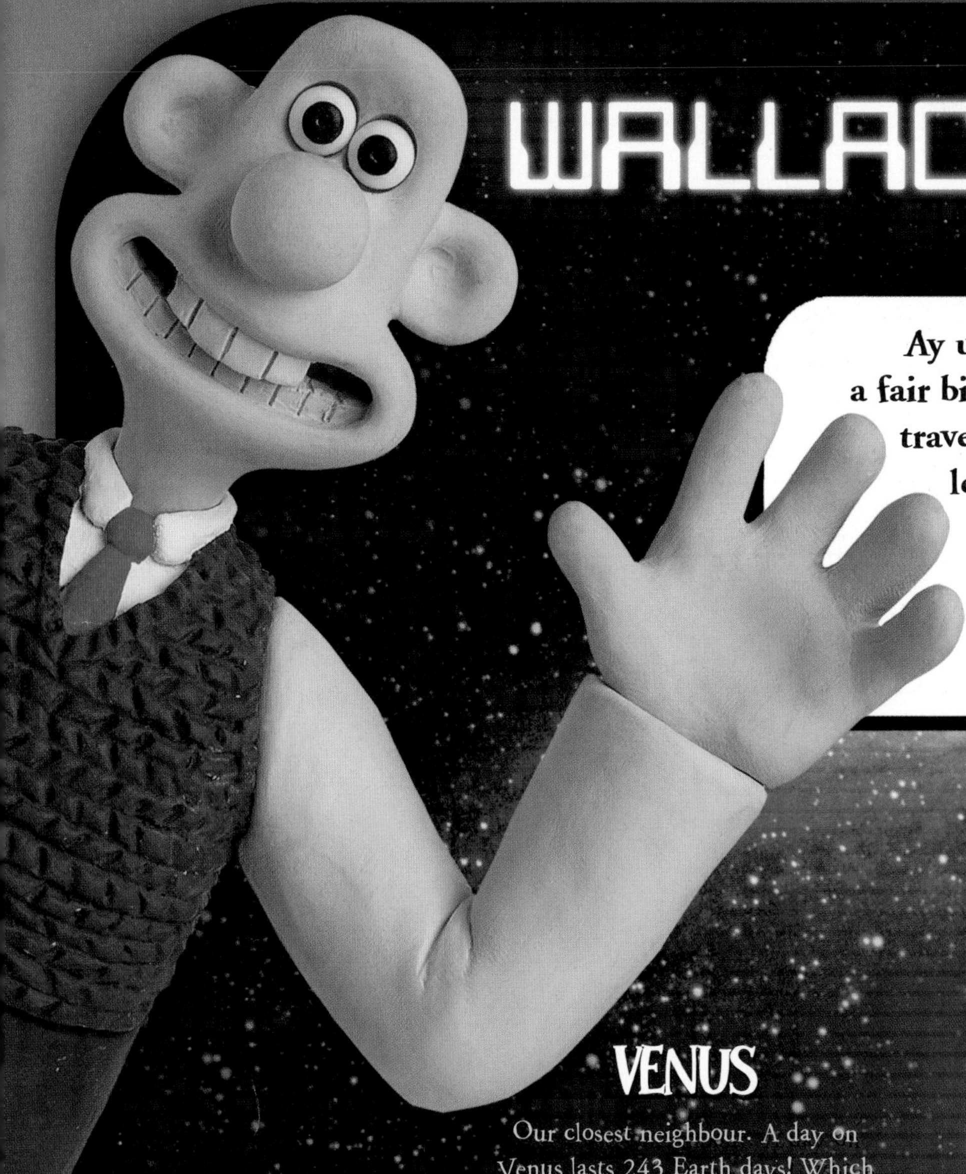

Ay up! The lad and myself have had a fair bit of experience with interplanetary travel (well, we've been to the Moon at least), so we thought we'd share the benefits of our wisdom. After all, it's always best to be prepared when visiting new places – or in this case, strange new worlds...

MARS

The red planet – or, as I like to call it, the Red Leicester planet. With its giant canyons, Mars is home to some of the most spectacular scenery in the Solar System – alongside the Yorkshire dales, of course!

VENUS

Our closest neighbour. A day on Venus lasts 243 Earth days! Which makes it an ideal spot to tackle that weighty tome you've been putting off – like the *Bumper Book of Cheese Facts: Revised, Annotated Edition.*

MERCURY

The nearest planet to the Sun. The temperature on Mercury ranges from -170°C at night to 350°C during the day. So it's best to take one of Wendolene's big scarves for those chilly evenings, and a pan for breakfast in the morning – instant fry-up when the sun rises!

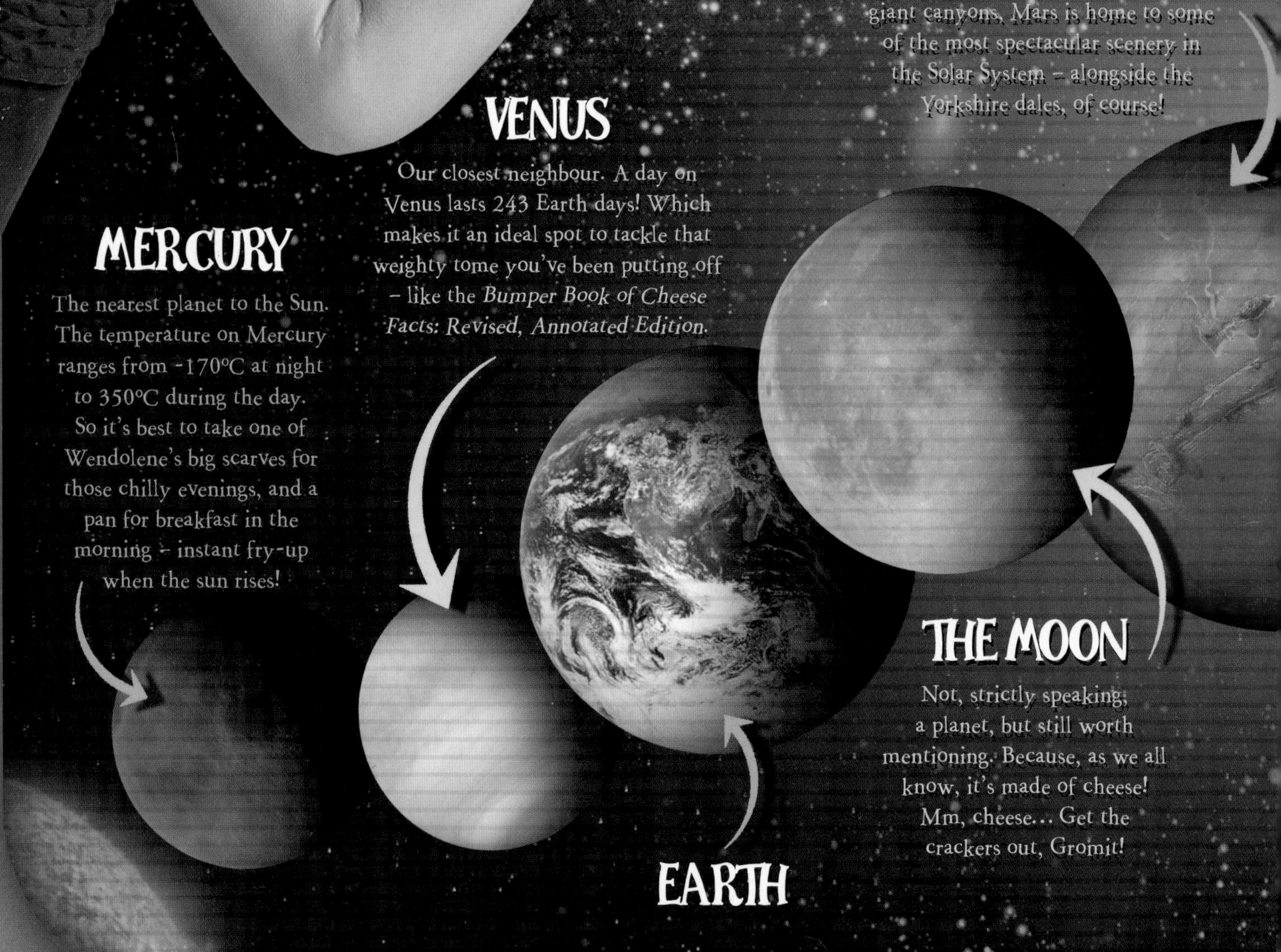

THE MOON

Not, strictly speaking, a planet, but still worth mentioning. Because, as we all know, it's made of cheese! Mm, cheese... Get the crackers out, Gromit!

EARTH

TO THE SOLAR SYSTEM

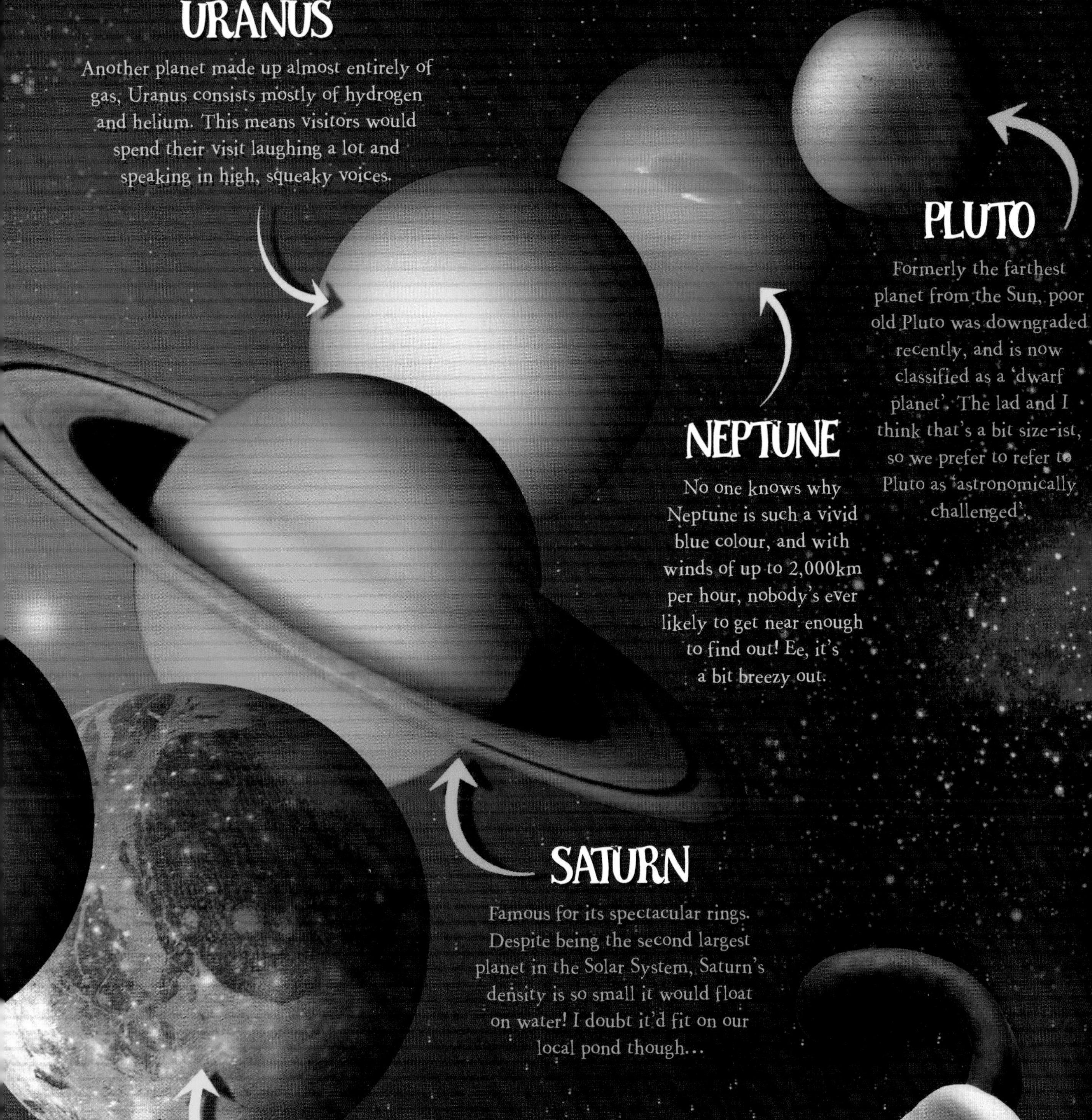

URANUS

Another planet made up almost entirely of gas, Uranus consists mostly of hydrogen and helium. This means visitors would spend their visit laughing a lot and speaking in high, squeaky voices.

PLUTO

Formerly the farthest planet from the Sun, poor old Pluto was downgraded recently, and is now classified as a 'dwarf planet'. The lad and I think that's a bit size-ist, so we prefer to refer to Pluto as 'astronomically challenged'.

NEPTUNE

No one knows why Neptune is such a vivid blue colour, and with winds of up to 2,000km per hour, nobody's ever likely to get near enough to find out! Ee, it's a bit breezy out.

SATURN

Famous for its spectacular rings. Despite being the second largest planet in the Solar System, Saturn's density is so small it would float on water! I doubt it'd fit on our local pond though...

JUPITER

The biggest planet in our Solar System, Jupiter is larger than all the other planets put together! It's also composed almost entirely of gas, with a small core of solid rock – a bit like one of Gromit's soufflés.

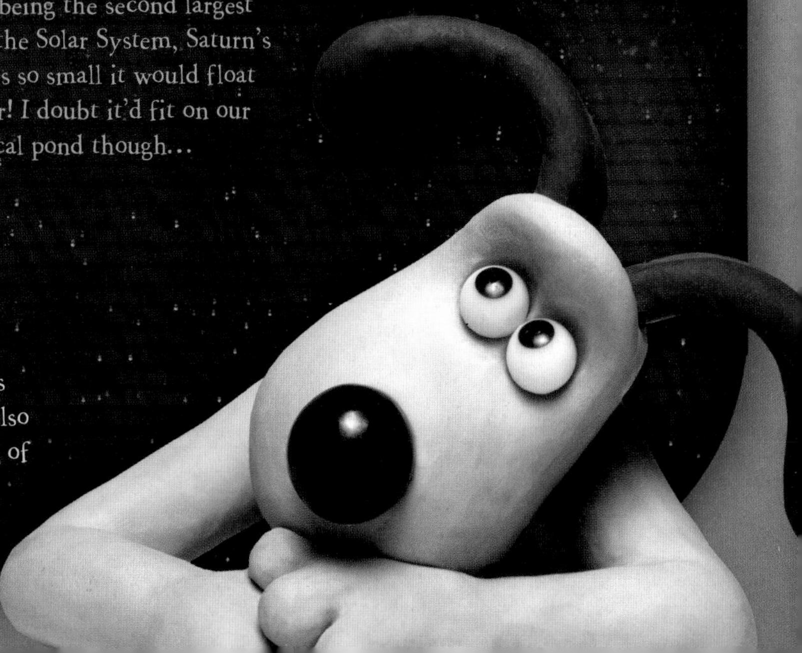

Dear Wallace,

On behalf of the Inventors' Guild, and in recognition of your tireless efforts
on behalf of the project, I am tickled pink to extend an invitation to you (and
Gromit) to visit R.A.D.I.S.H. (RESEARCH ALLOTMENT DEPLOYED ON
INTERNATIONAL SPACE HUB). After a few last operational hiccups, the
orbital platform is now fully operational, and we can confidently predict plain
sailing from here on in.

Pop up and see us anytime (no need to call ahead). We've mammoth marrows,
bumper beets, colossal cabbages and oversized okra... all ready for sampling.
And if you've room on the return journey, I'm sure your good friend Lady
Tottington would relish our titanic tomatoes. Look forward to seeing you (and
Gromit) soon.

Best regards,

Heywood

Heywood Gardengates, IE, DVD, IQ & FT

PS: your meteor-swatter has already proved invaluable, saving us from
several careening comets and a rogue asteroid.

PPS: it also makes a great zero gravity swingball bat!

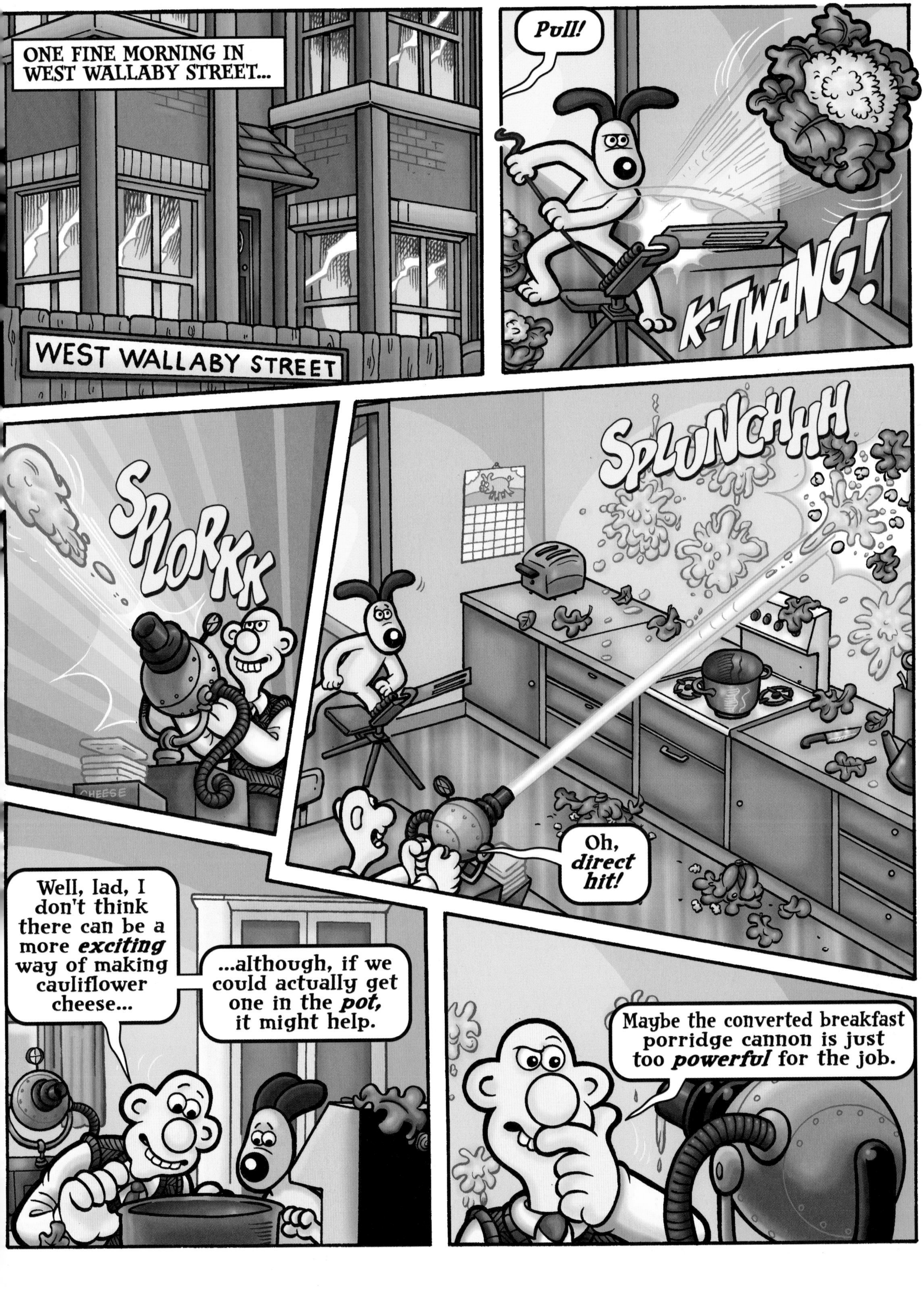

ONE FINE MORNING IN WEST WALLABY STREET...
WEST WALLABY STREET
Pull!
K-TWANG!
SPLORKK
CHEESE
SPLUNCHHH
Oh, direct hit!
Well, lad, I don't think there can be a more exciting way of making cauliflower cheese...
...although, if we could actually get one in the pot, it might help.
Maybe the converted breakfast porridge cannon is just too powerful for the job.

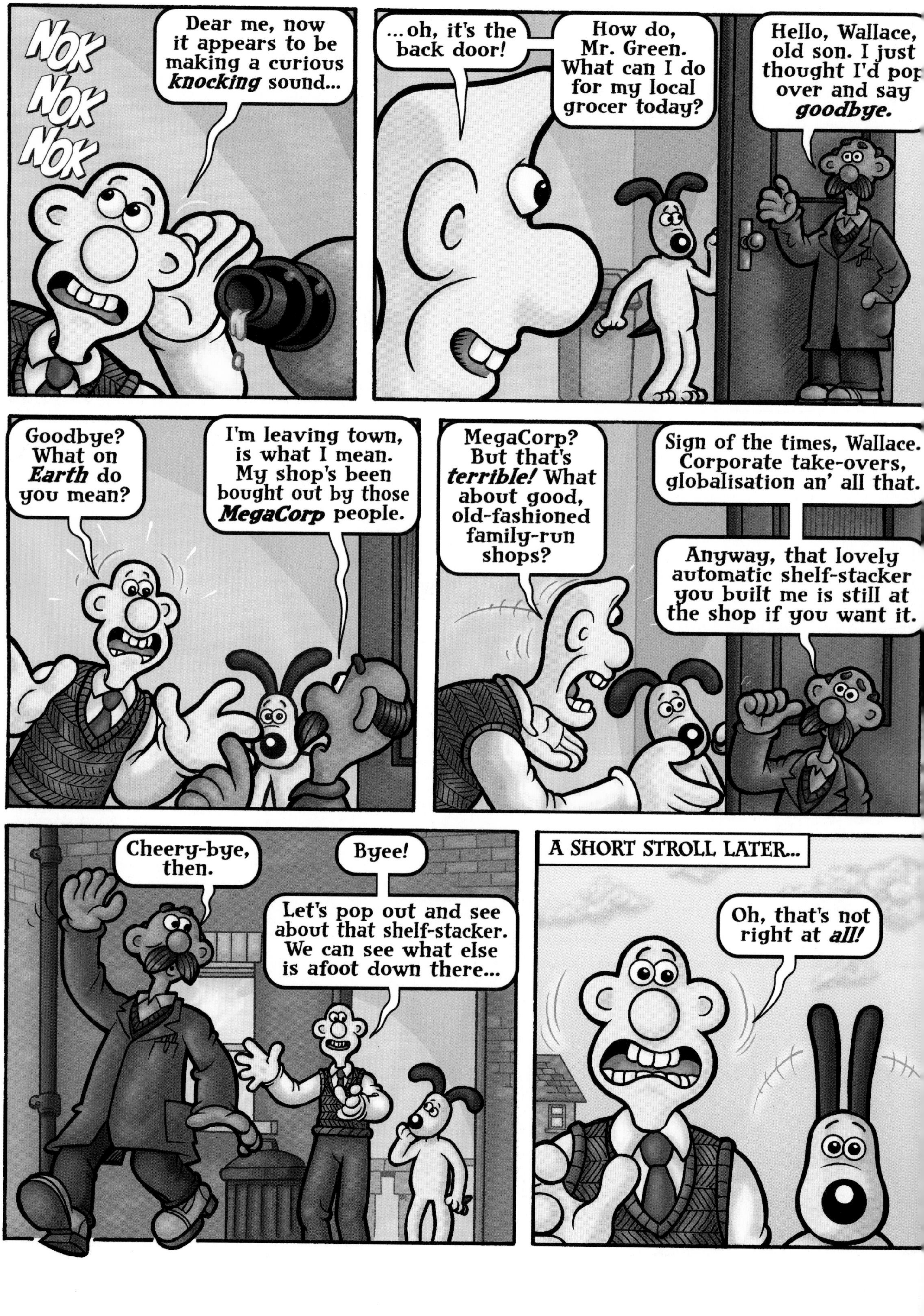
NOK NOK NOK
Dear me, now it appears to be making a curious *knocking* sound...
...oh, it's the back door!
How do, Mr. Green. What can I do for my local grocer today?
Hello, Wallace, old son. I just thought I'd pop over and say *goodbye.*
Goodbye? What on *Earth* do you mean?
I'm leaving town, is what I mean. My shop's been bought out by those *MegaCorp* people.
MegaCorp? But that's *terrible!* What about good, old-fashioned family-run shops?
Sign of the times, Wallace. Corporate take-overs, globalisation an' all that.
Anyway, that lovely automatic shelf-stacker you built me is still at the shop if you want it.
Cheery-bye, then.
Byee!
Let's pop out and see about that shelf-stacker. We can see what else is afoot down there...
A SHORT STROLL LATER...
Oh, that's not right at *all!*

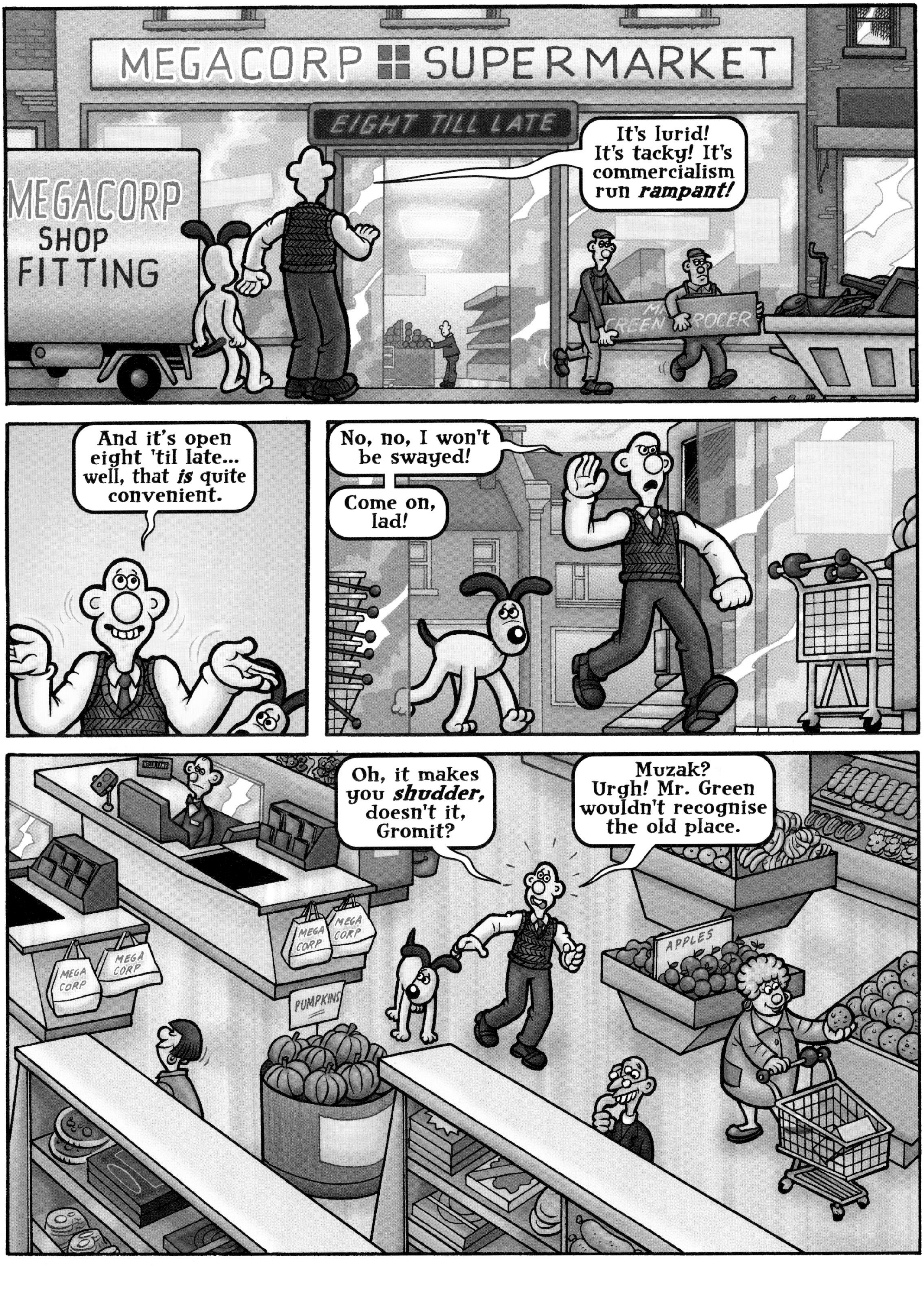
MEGACORP SUPERMARKET
EIGHT TILL LATE
MEGACORP SHOP FITTING
It's lurid! It's tacky! It's commercialism run *rampant!*
And it's open eight 'til late... well, that *is* quite convenient.
No, no, I won't be swayed!
Come on, lad!
MEGA CORP
PUMPKINS
APPLES
Oh, it makes you *shudder,* doesn't it, Gromit?
Muzak? Urgh! Mr. Green wouldn't recognise the old place.

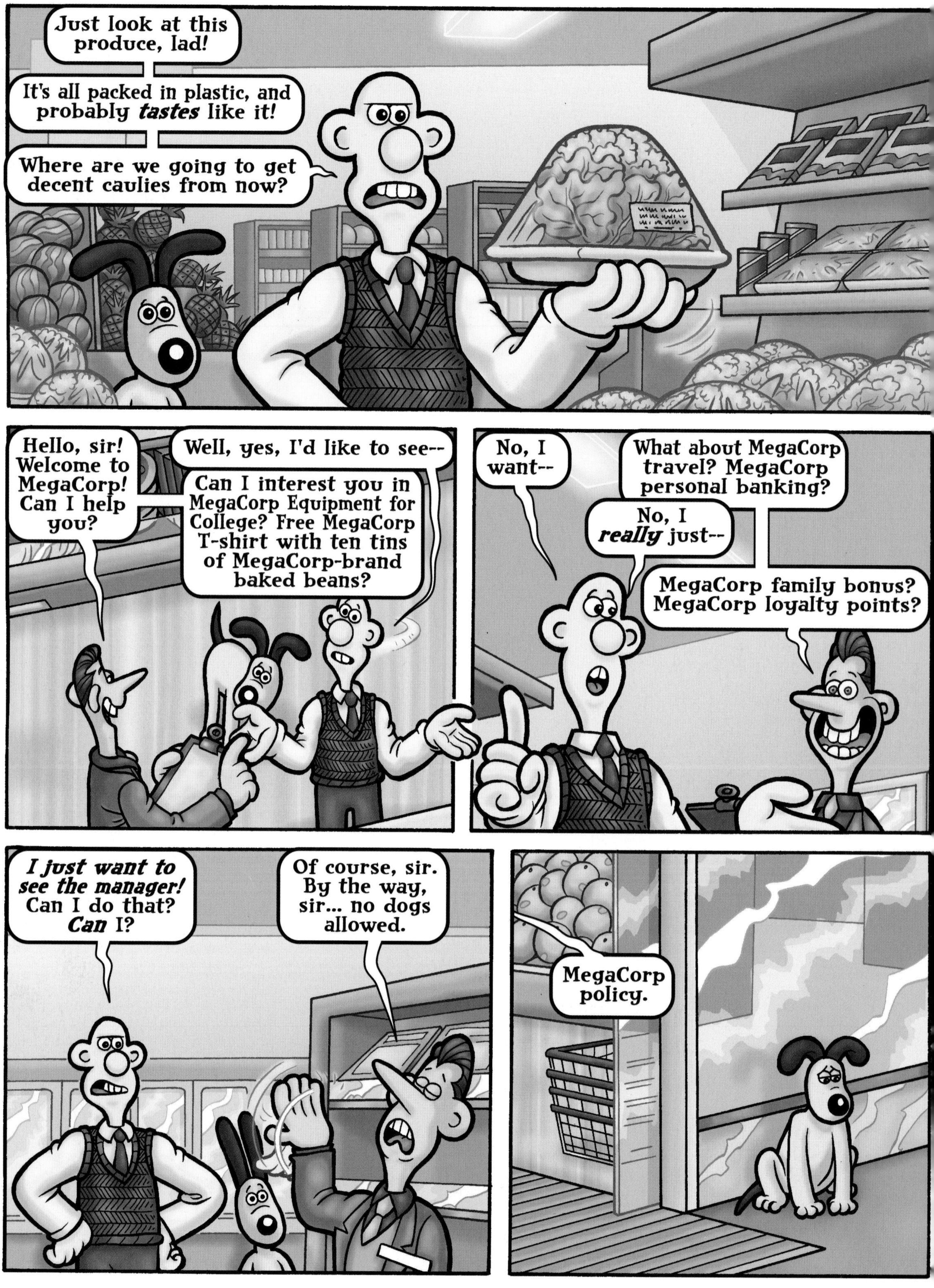

Just look at this produce, lad!
It's all packed in plastic, and probably *tastes* like it!
Where are we going to get decent caulies from now?
Hello, sir! Welcome to MegaCorp! Can I help you?
Well, yes, I'd like to see--
Can I interest you in MegaCorp Equipment for College? Free MegaCorp T-shirt with ten tins of MegaCorp-brand baked beans?
No, I want--
What about MegaCorp travel? MegaCorp personal banking?
No, I *really* just--
MegaCorp family bonus? MegaCorp loyalty points?
I just want to see the manager! Can I do that? *Can* I?
Of course, sir. By the way, sir... no dogs allowed.
MegaCorp policy.

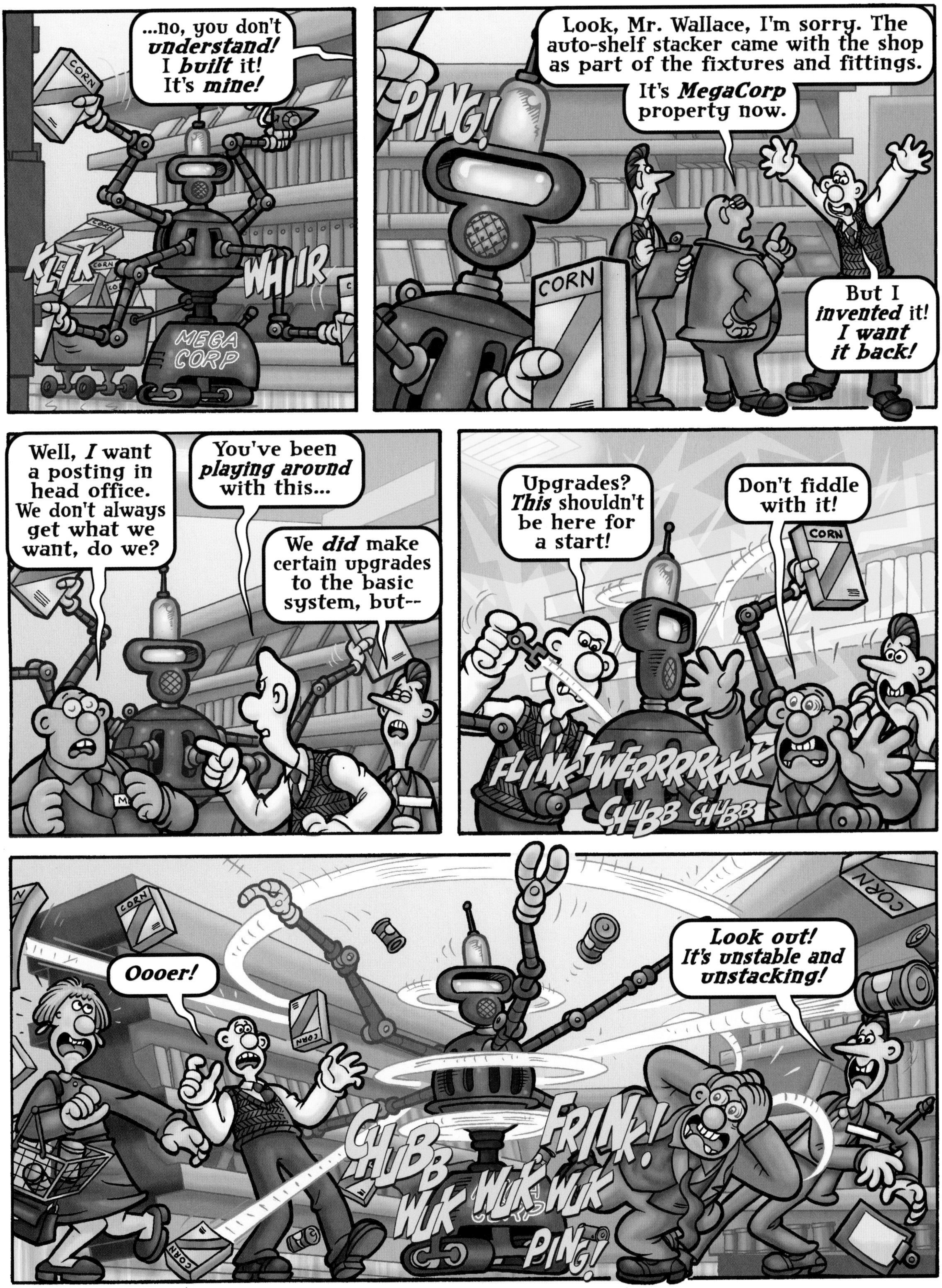

...no, you don't *understand!* I *built* it! It's *mine!*
CORN
KLIK
WHIIR
MEGA CORP
Look, Mr. Wallace, I'm sorry. The auto-shelf stacker came with the shop as part of the fixtures and fittings.
It's *MegaCorp* property now.
PING!
CORN
But I *invented* it! *I want it back!*
Well, *I* want a posting in head office. We don't always get what we want, do we?
You've been *playing around* with this...
We *did* make certain upgrades to the basic system, but--
Upgrades? *This* shouldn't be here for a start!
Don't fiddle with it!
CORN
FLINK
TWERRRRKKK
CHUBB CHUBB
CORN
Oooer!
Look out! It's unstable and unstacking!
CHUBB
FRINK!
WUK WUK WUK
PING!

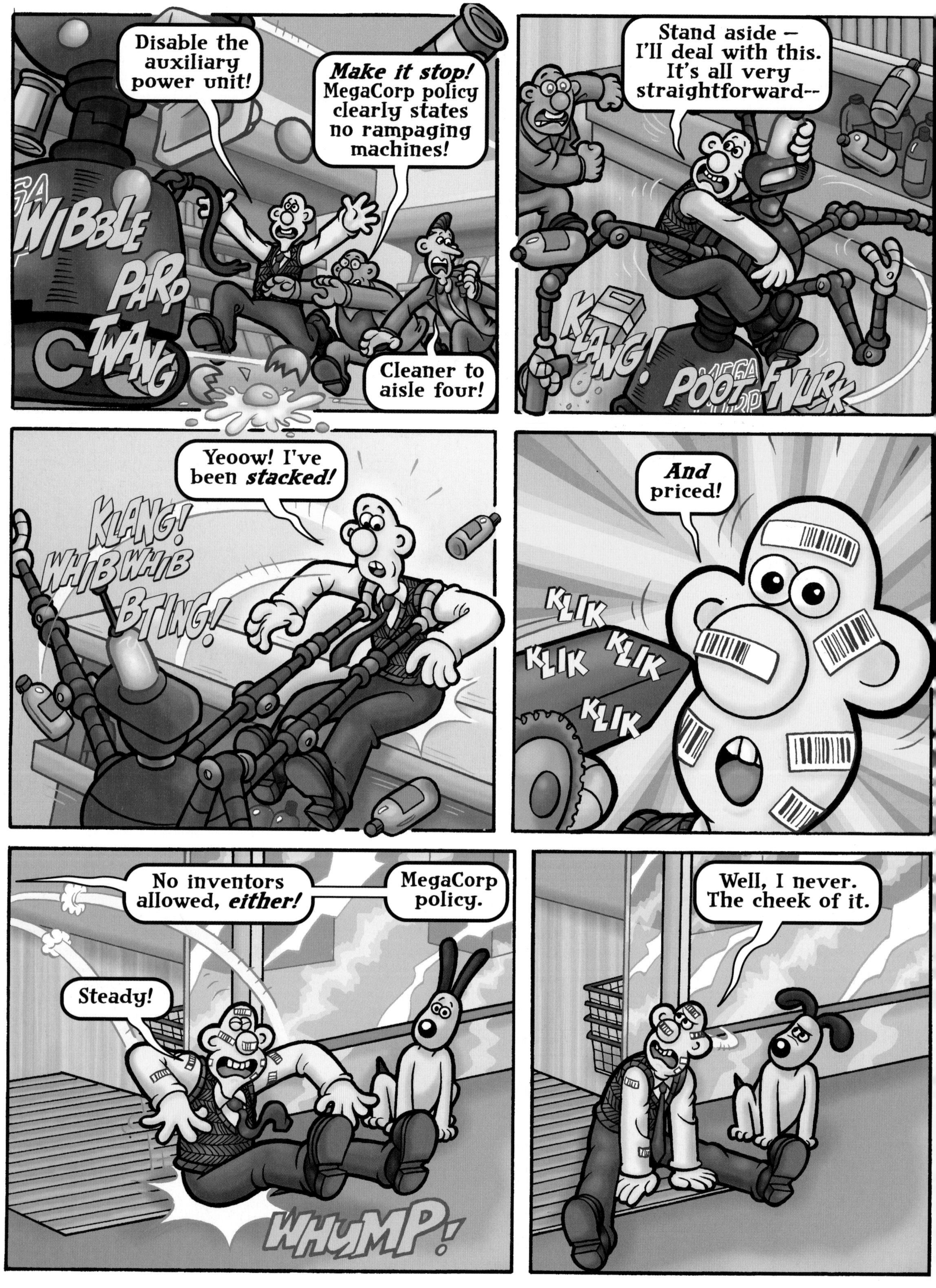

Disable the auxiliary power unit!
Make it stop! MegaCorp policy clearly states no rampaging machines!
WIBBLE
PARP
TWANG
Cleaner to aisle four!
Stand aside – I'll deal with this. It's all very straightforward--
KLANG!
POOT
FNURK
Yeoow! I've been stacked!
KLANG!
WHIB WHIB
BTING!
And priced!
KLIK
KLIK
KLIK
KLIK
No inventors allowed, either!
MegaCorp policy.
Steady!
WHUMP!
Well, I never. The cheek of it.

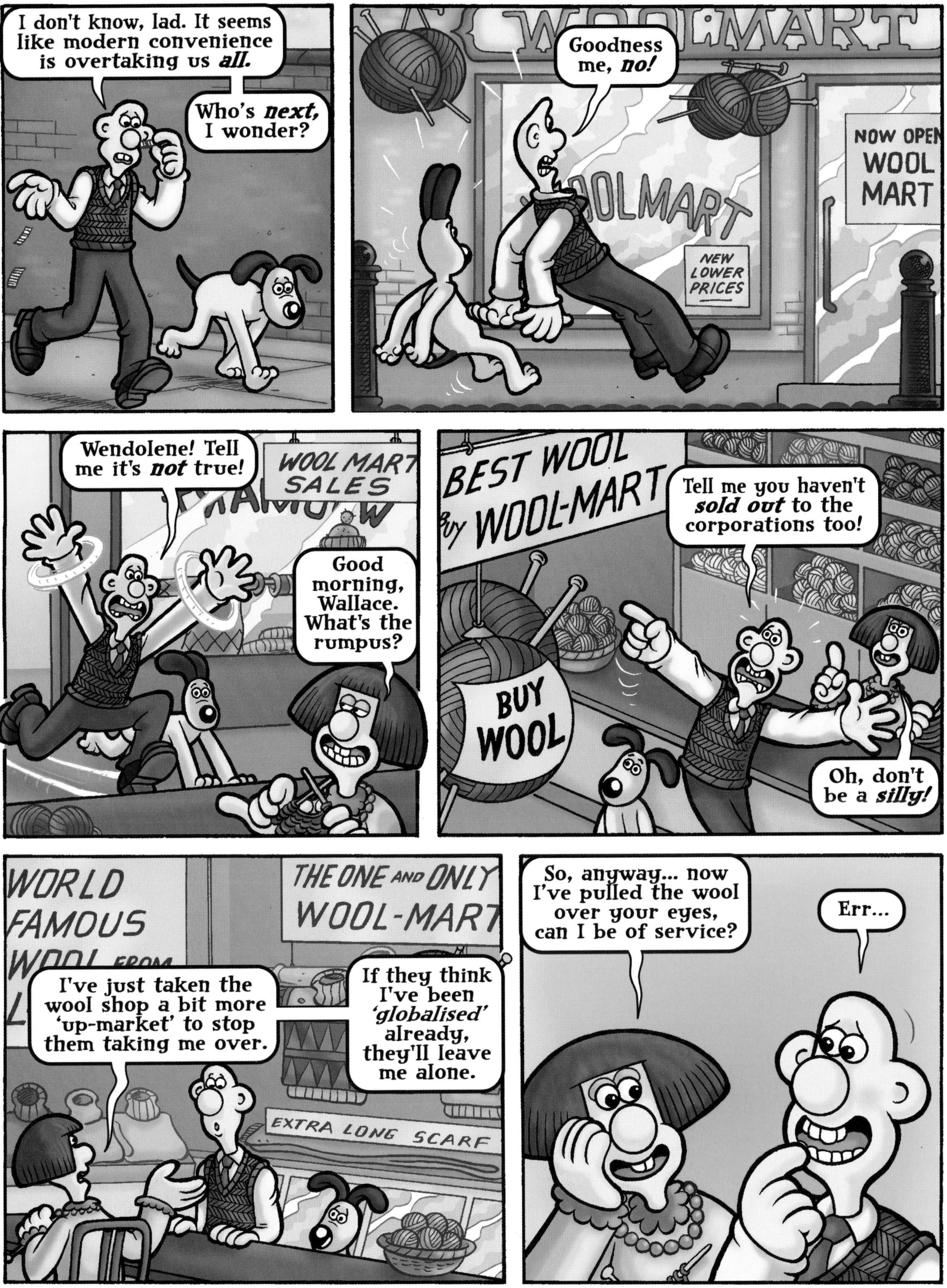

I don't know, lad. It seems like modern convenience is overtaking us *all.*
Who's *next,* I wonder?
WOOLMART
Goodness me, *no!*
WOOLMART
NOW OPEN WOOL MART
NEW LOWER PRICES
Wendolene! Tell me it's *not* true!
WOOL MART SALES
Good morning, Wallace. What's the rumpus?
BEST WOOL BUY WOOL-MART
Tell me you haven't *sold out* to the corporations too!
BUY WOOL
Oh, don't be a *silly!*
WORLD FAMOUS
THE ONE AND ONLY WOOL-MART
I've just taken the wool shop a bit more 'up-market' to stop them taking me over.
If they think I've been *'globalised'* already, they'll leave me alone.
EXTRA LONG SCARF
So, anyway... now I've pulled the wool over your eyes, can I be of service?
Err...

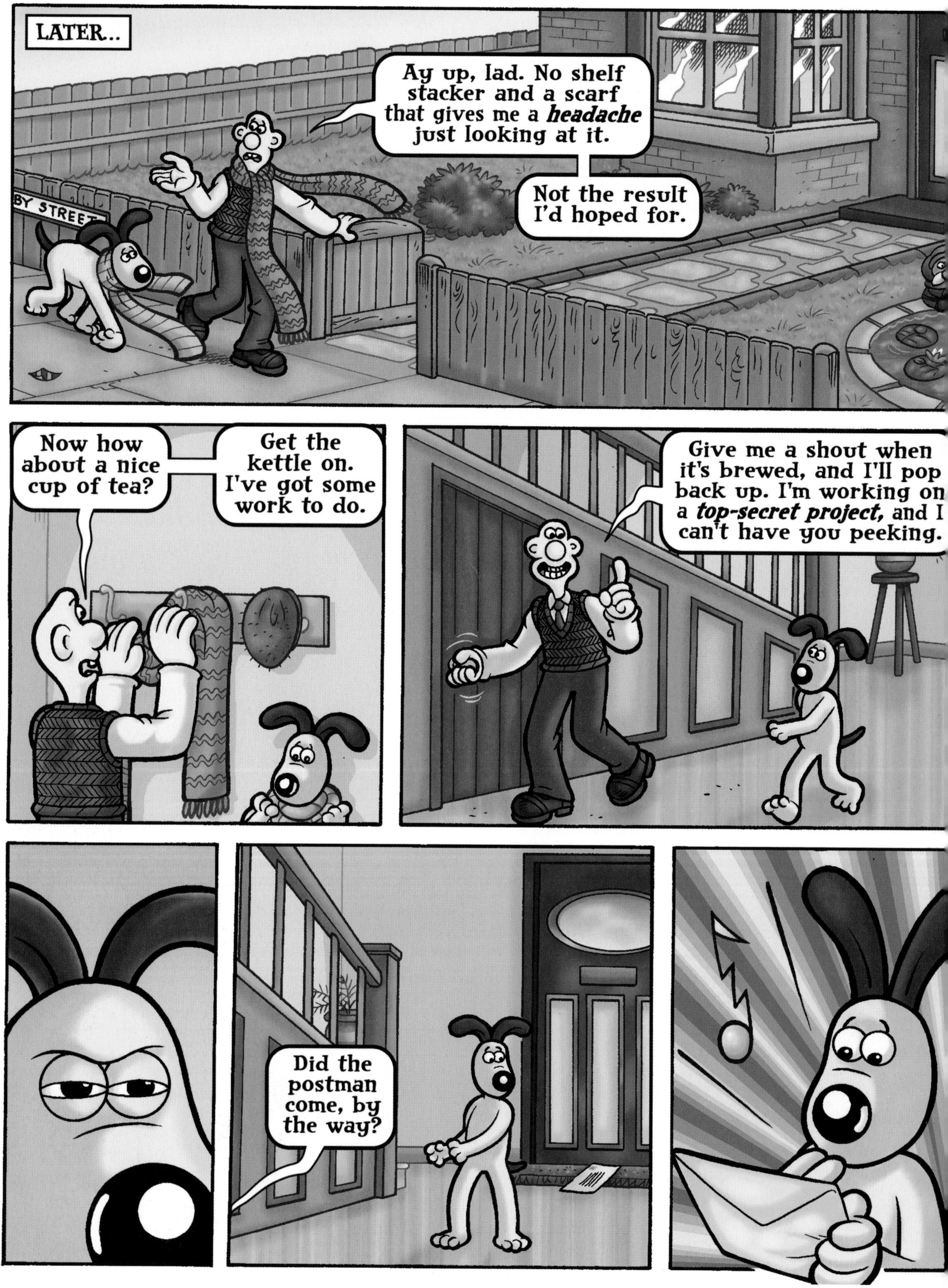

LATER...
Ay up, lad. No shelf stacker and a scarf that gives me a *headache* just looking at it.
Not the result I'd hoped for.
BY STREET
Now how about a nice cup of tea?
Get the kettle on. I've got some work to do.
Give me a shout when it's brewed, and I'll pop back up. I'm working on a *top-secret project,* and I can't have you peeking.
Did the postman come, by the way?

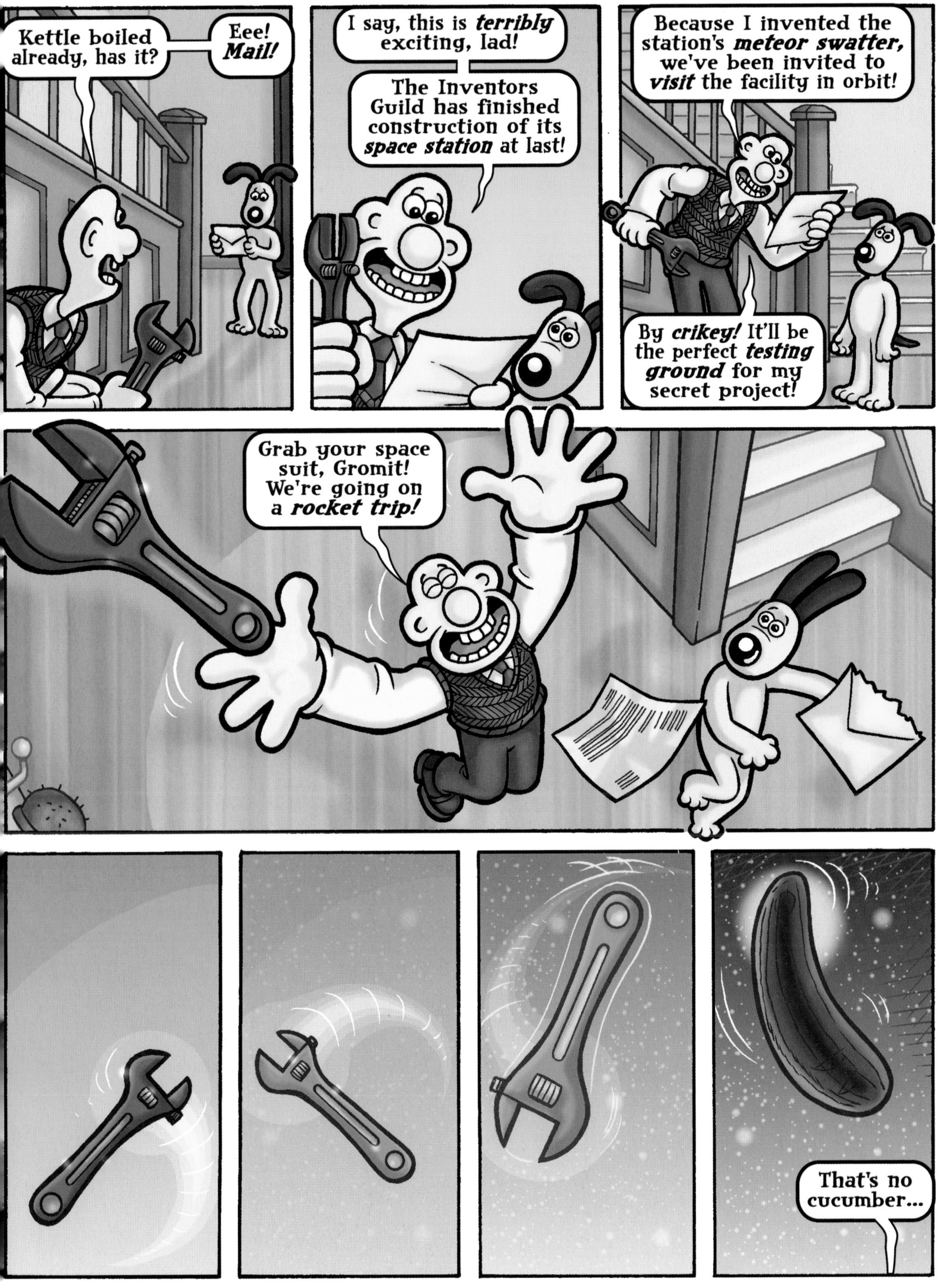

Kettle boiled already, has it?
Eee! *Mail!*
I say, this is *terribly* exciting, lad!
The Inventors Guild has finished construction of its *space station* at last!
Because I invented the station's *meteor swatter,* we've been invited to *visit* the facility in orbit!
By *crikey!* It'll be the perfect *testing ground* for my secret project!
Grab your space suit, Gromit! We're going on a *rocket trip!*
That's no cucumber...

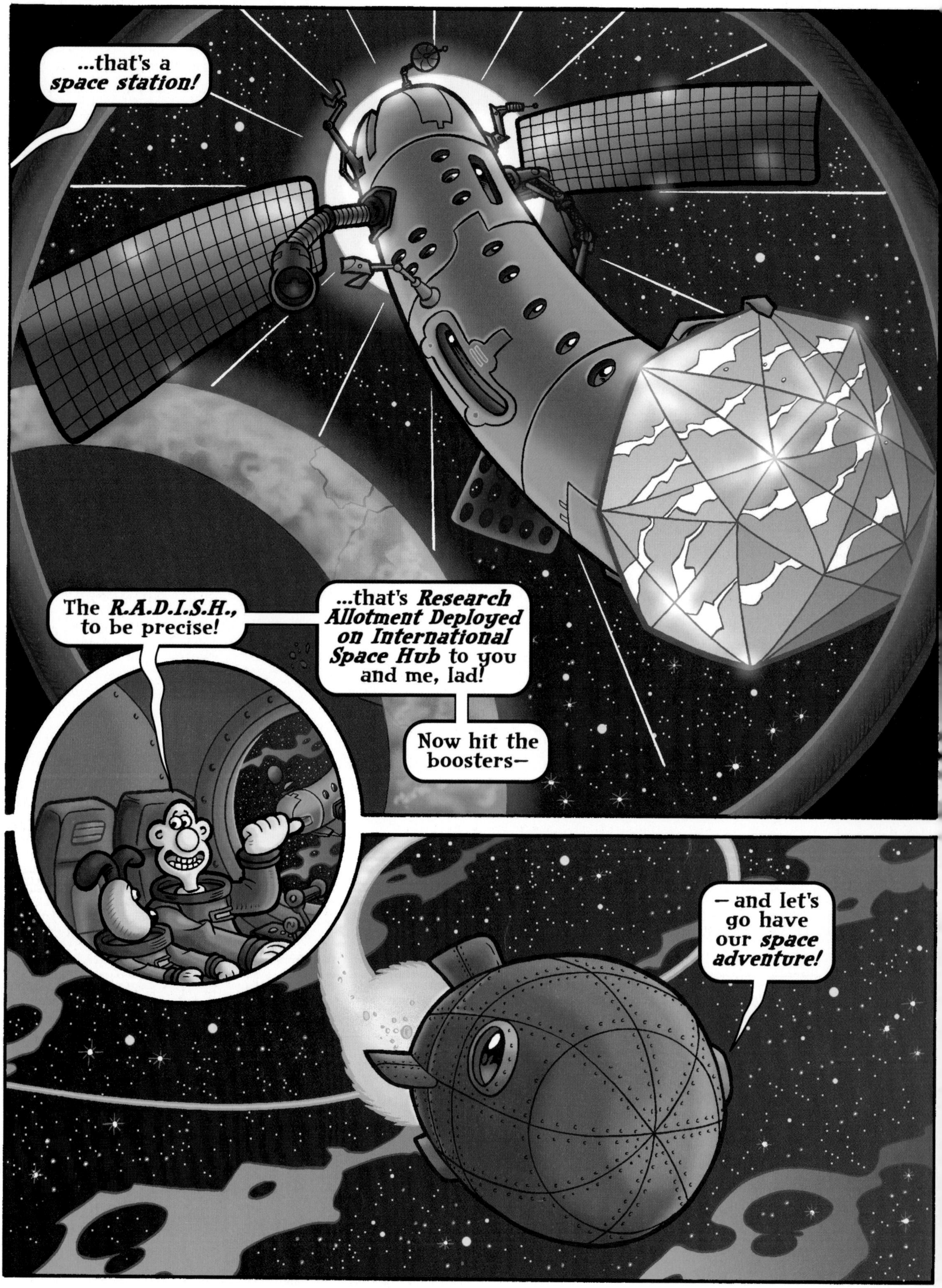
...that's a *space station!*
The *R.A.D.I.S.H.*, to be precise!
...that's *Research Allotment Deployed on International Space Hub* to you and me, lad!
Now hit the boosters—
— and let's go have our *space adventure!*

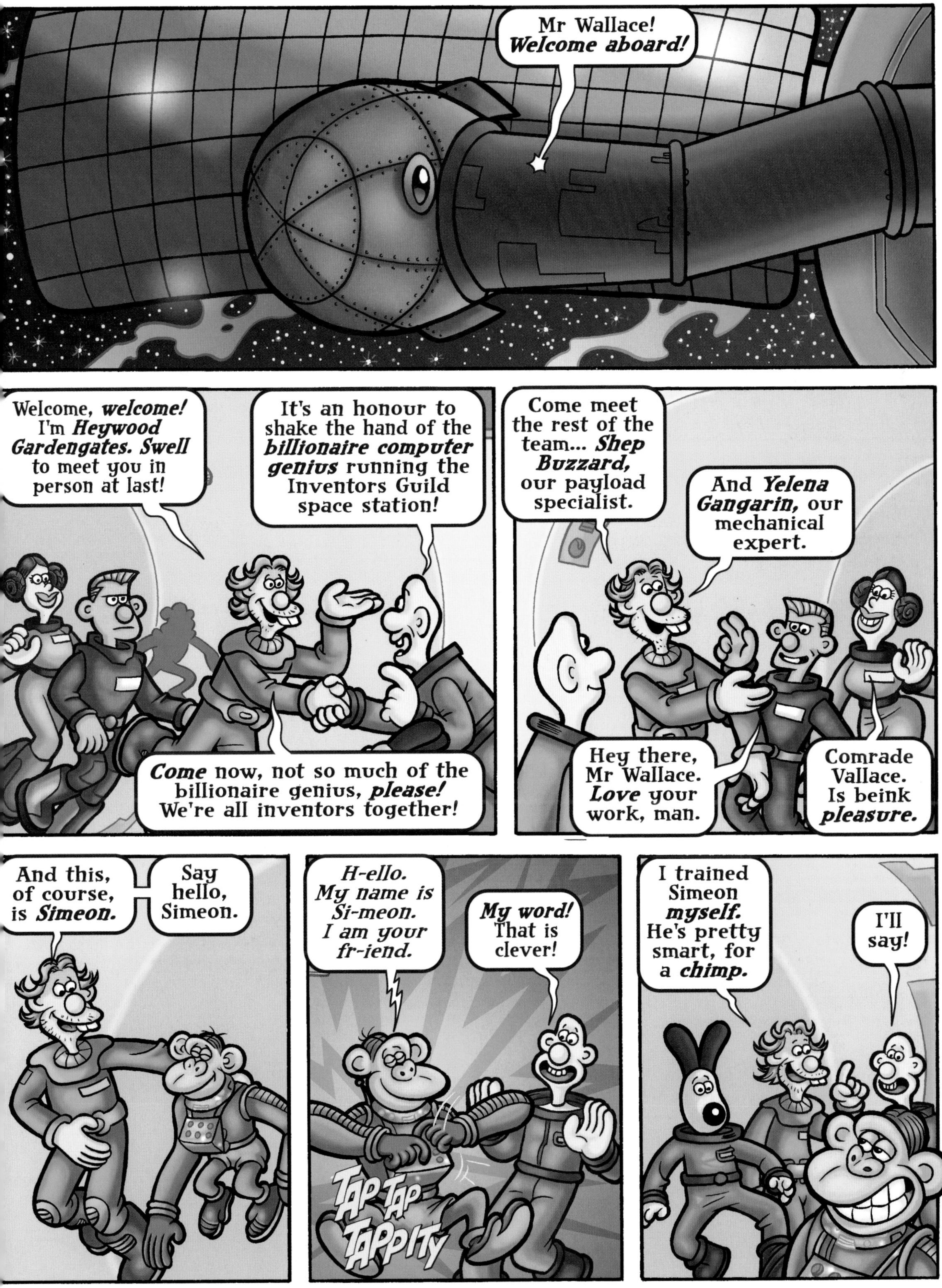
Mr Wallace! Welcome aboard!
Welcome, welcome! I'm Heywood Gardengates. Swell to meet you in person at last!
It's an honour to shake the hand of the billionaire computer genius running the Inventors Guild space station!
Come now, not so much of the billionaire genius, please! We're all inventors together!
Come meet the rest of the team... Shep Buzzard, our payload specialist.
And Yelena Gangarin, our mechanical expert.
Hey there, Mr Wallace. Love your work, man.
Comrade Vallace. Is beink pleasure.
And this, of course, is Simeon.
Say hello, Simeon.
H-ello. My name is Si-meon. I am your fr-iend.
My word! That is clever!
TAP TAP TAPPITY
I trained Simeon myself. He's pretty smart, for a chimp.
I'll say!

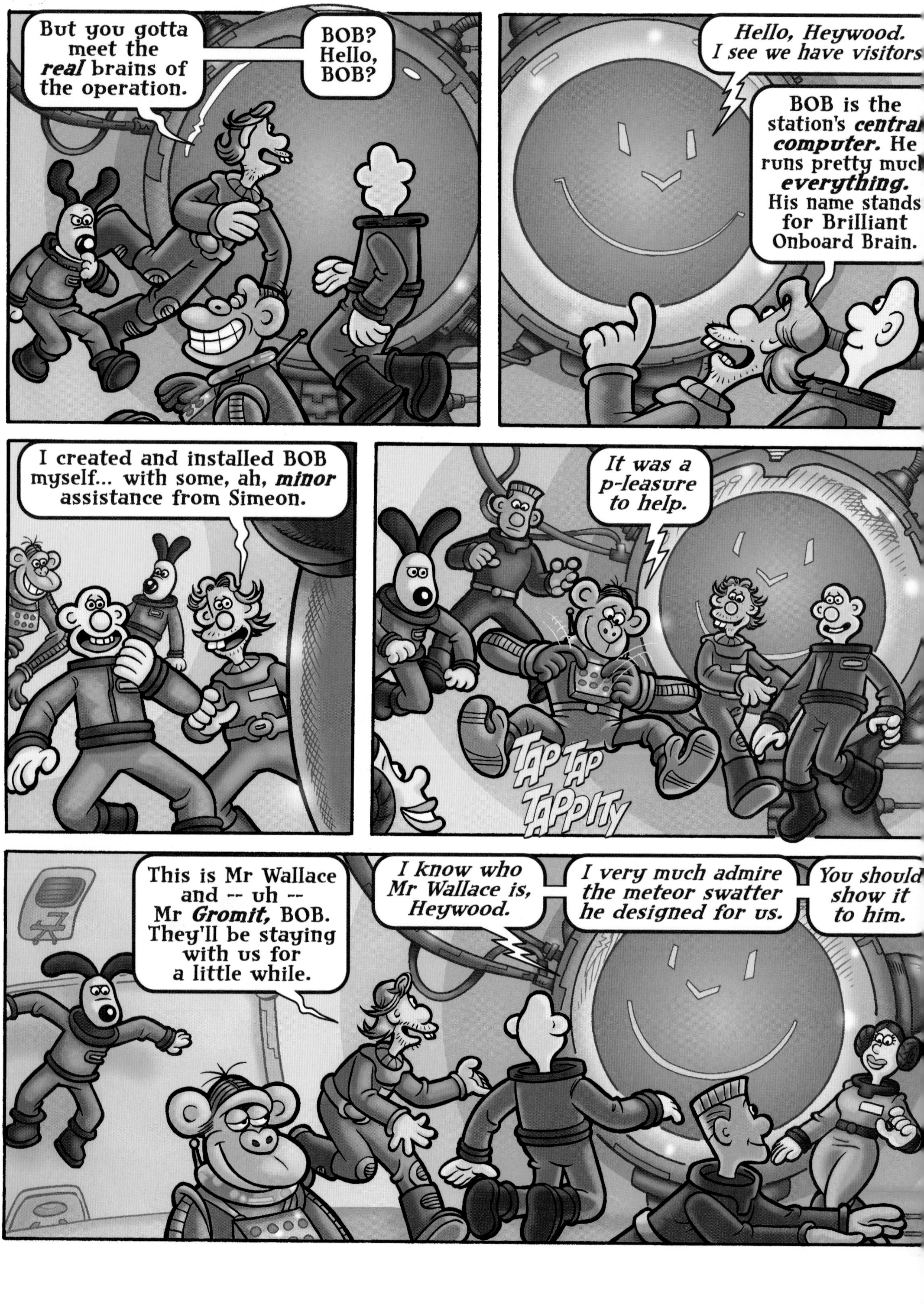

But you gotta meet the *real* brains of the operation.
BOB? Hello, BOB?
Hello, Heywood. I see we have visitors
BOB is the station's ***central computer.*** He runs pretty much ***everything.*** His name stands for Brilliant Onboard Brain.
I created and installed BOB myself... with some, ah, ***minor*** assistance from Simeon.
It was a p-leasure to help.
TAP TAP TAPPITY
This is Mr Wallace and -- uh -- Mr ***Gromit,*** BOB. They'll be staying with us for a little while.
I know who Mr Wallace is, Heywood.
I very much admire the meteor swatter he designed for us.
You should show it to him.

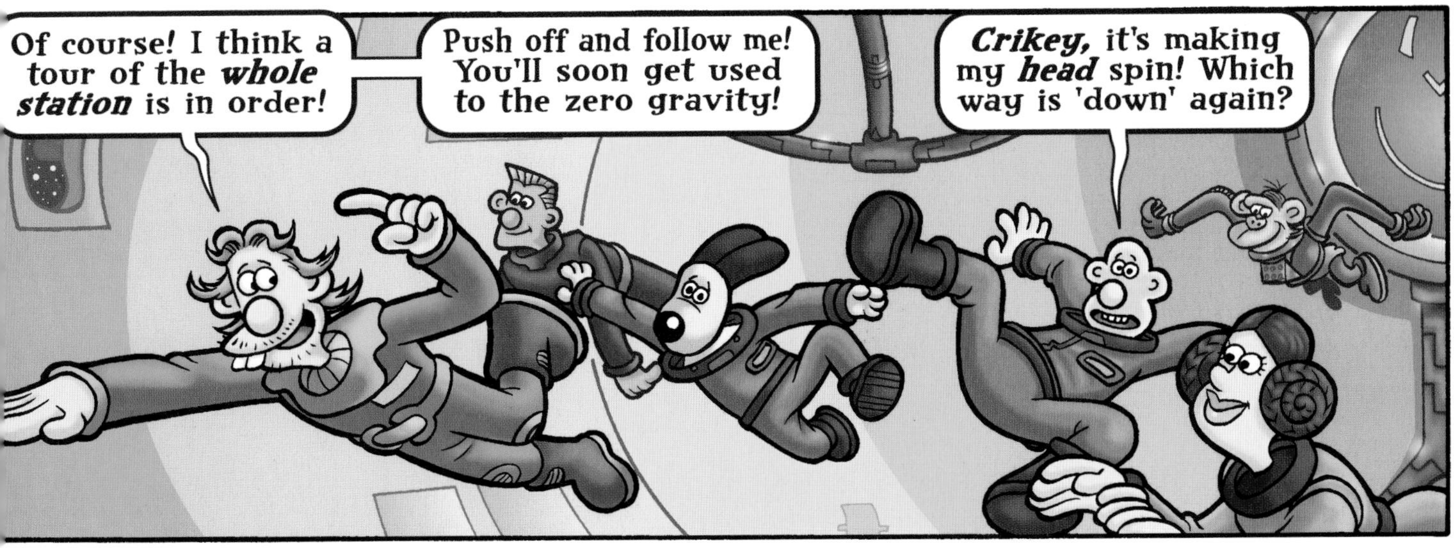
Of course! I think a tour of the *whole station* is in order!
Push off and follow me! You'll soon get used to the zero gravity!
Crikey, it's making my *head* spin! Which way is 'down' again?

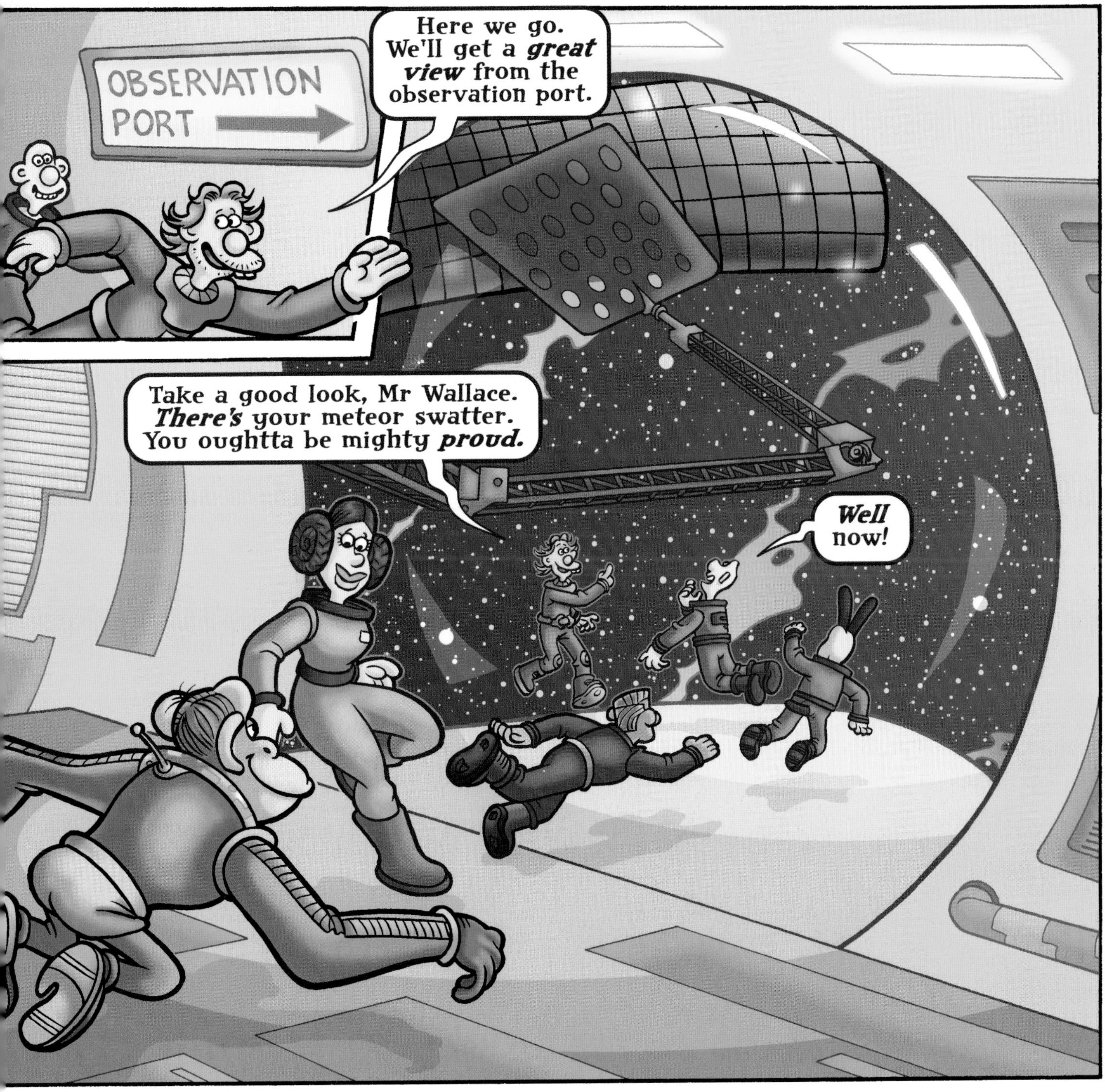
OBSERVATION PORT
Here we go. We'll get a *great view* from the observation port.
Take a good look, Mr Wallace. *There's* your meteor swatter. You oughtta be mighty *proud.*
Well now!

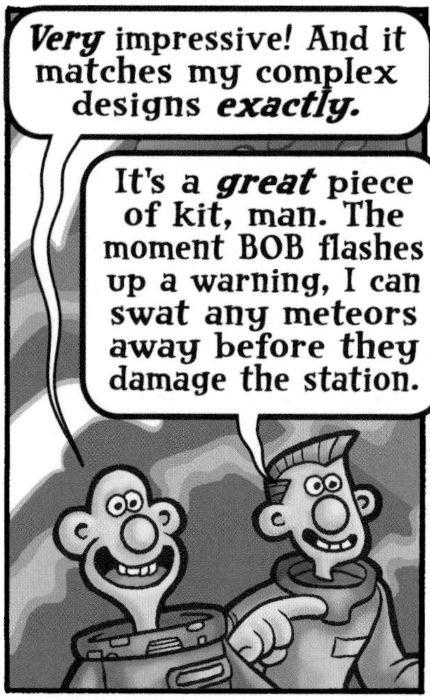
Very impressive! And it matches my complex designs *exactly.*
It's a *great* piece of kit, man. The moment BOB flashes up a warning, I can swat any meteors away before they damage the station.

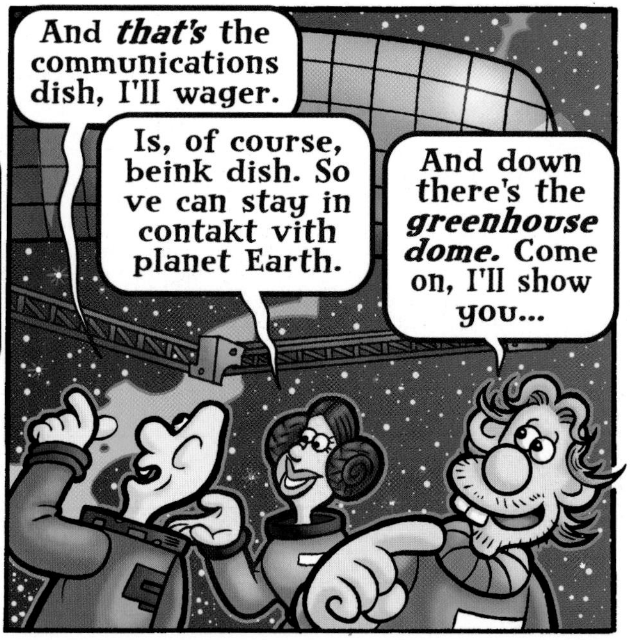
And *that's* the communications dish, I'll wager.
Is, of course, beink dish. So ve can stay in contakt vith planet Earth.
And down there's the *greenhouse dome.* Come on, I'll show you...

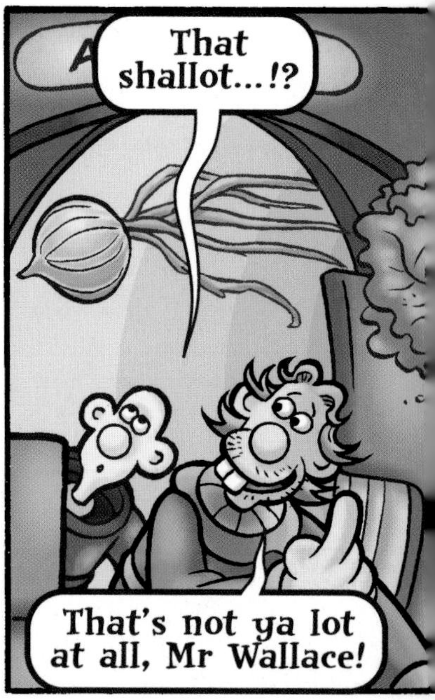
That shallot...!?
That's not ya lot at all, Mr Wallace!

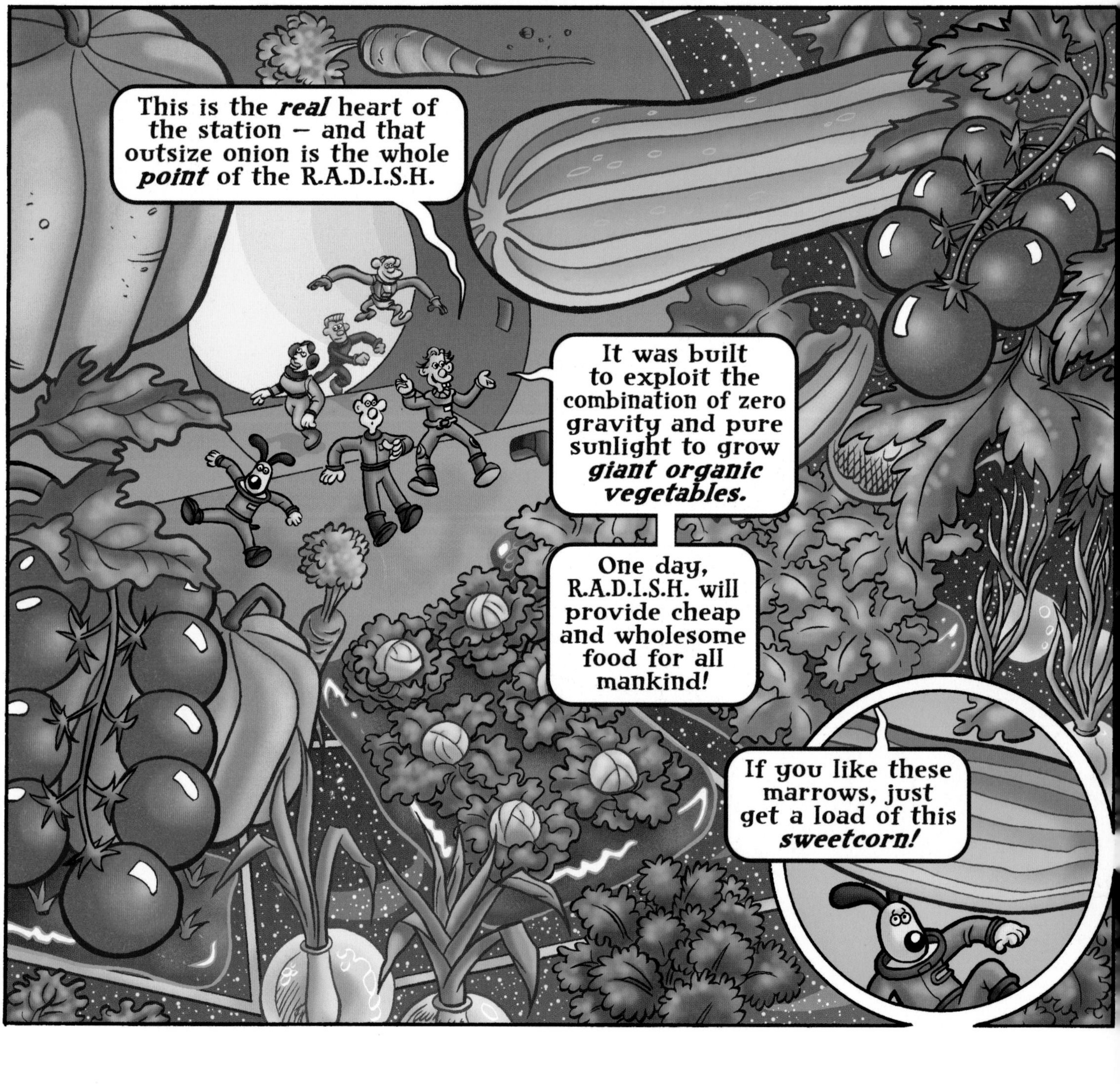
This is the *real* heart of the station – and that outsize onion is the whole *point* of the R.A.D.I.S.H.
It was built to exploit the combination of zero gravity and pure sunlight to grow *giant organic vegetables.*
One day, R.A.D.I.S.H. will provide cheap and wholesome food for all mankind!
If you like these marrows, just get a load of this *sweetcorn!*

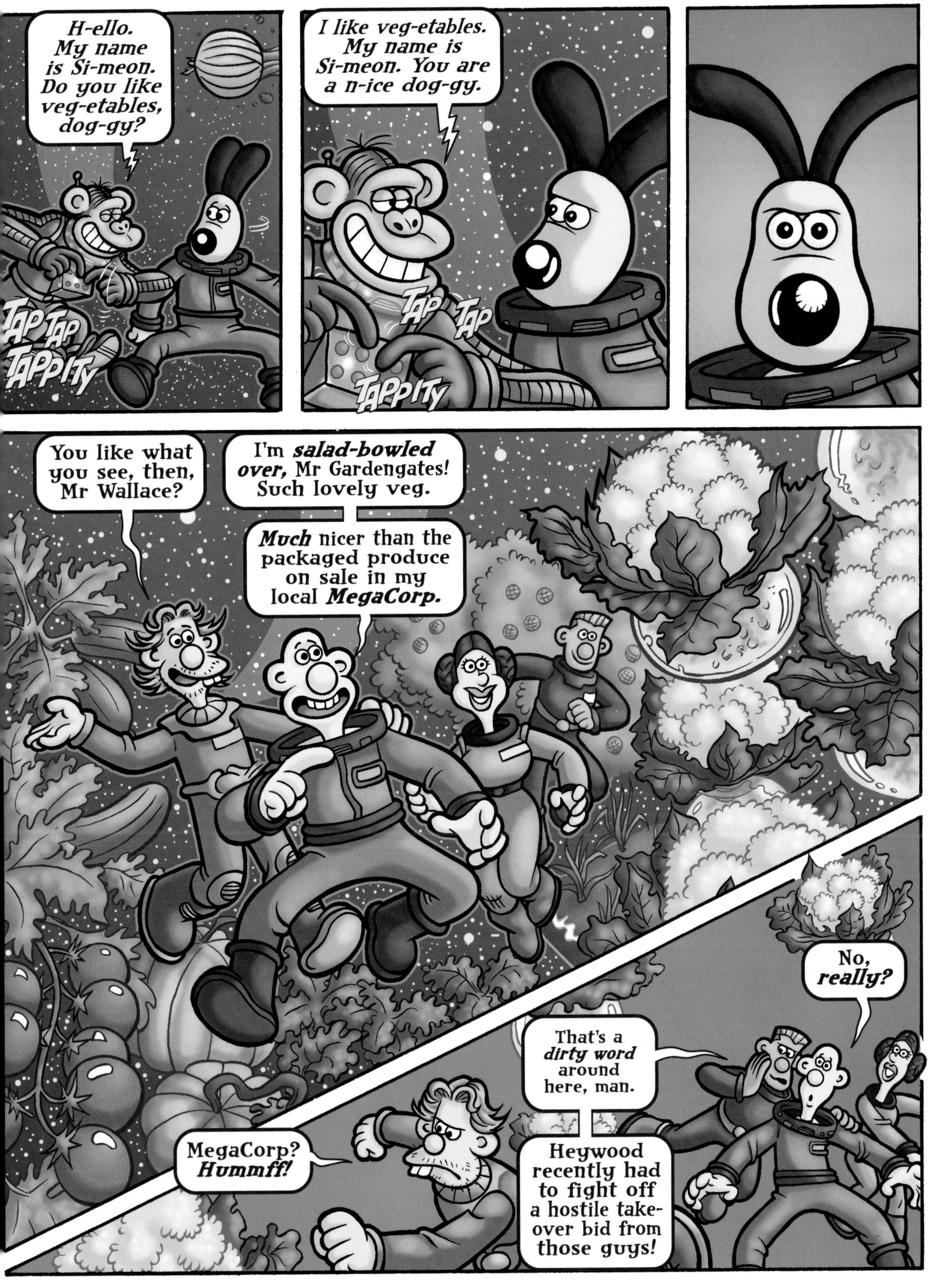
H-ello. My name is Si-meon. Do you like veg-etables, dog-gy?
TAP TAP TAPPITY
I like veg-etables. My name is Si-meon. You are a n-ice dog-gy.
TAP TAP TAPPITY
You like what you see, then, Mr Wallace?
I'm *salad-bowled over,* Mr Gardengates! Such lovely veg.
Much nicer than the packaged produce on sale in my local *MegaCorp.*
MegaCorp? *Hummff!*
That's a *dirty word* around here, man.
No, *really?*
Heywood recently had to fight off a hostile take-over bid from those guys!

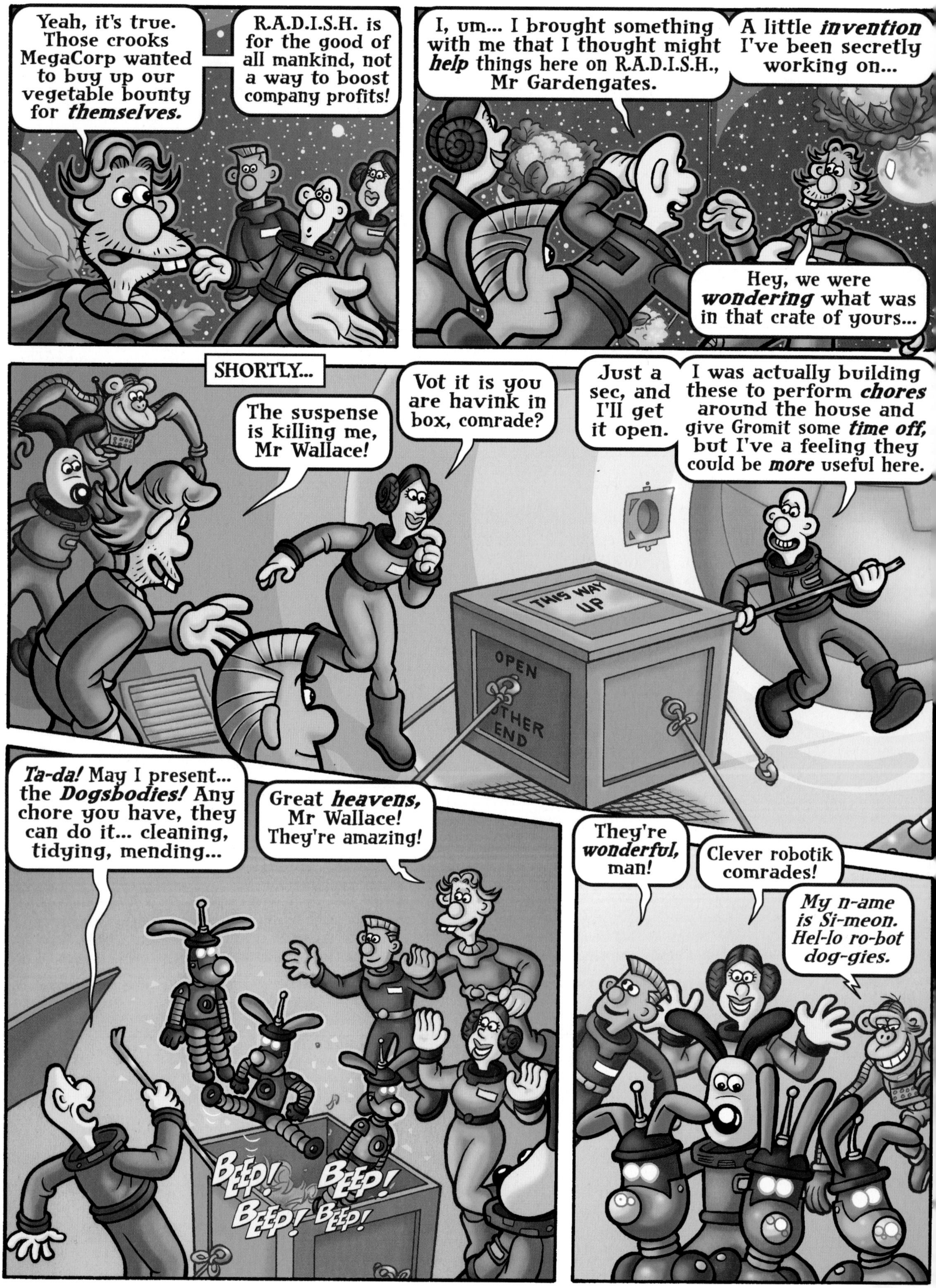
Yeah, it's true. Those crooks MegaCorp wanted to buy up our vegetable bounty for *themselves.*
R.A.D.I.S.H. is for the good of all mankind, not a way to boost company profits!
I, um... I brought something with me that I thought might *help* things here on R.A.D.I.S.H., Mr Gardengates.
A little *invention* I've been secretly working on...
Hey, we were *wondering* what was in that crate of yours...
SHORTLY...
The suspense is killing me, Mr Wallace!
Vot it is you are havink in box, comrade?
Just a sec, and I'll get it open.
I was actually building these to perform *chores* around the house and give Gromit some *time off,* but I've a feeling they could be *more* useful here.
THIS WAY UP
OPEN OTHER END
Ta-da! May I present... the *Dogsbodies!* Any chore you have, they can do it... cleaning, tidying, mending...
Great *heavens,* Mr Wallace! They're amazing!
BEEP! BEEP! BEEP! BEEP!
They're *wonderful,* man!
Clever robotik comrades!
My n-ame is Si-meon. Hel-lo ro-bot dog-gies.

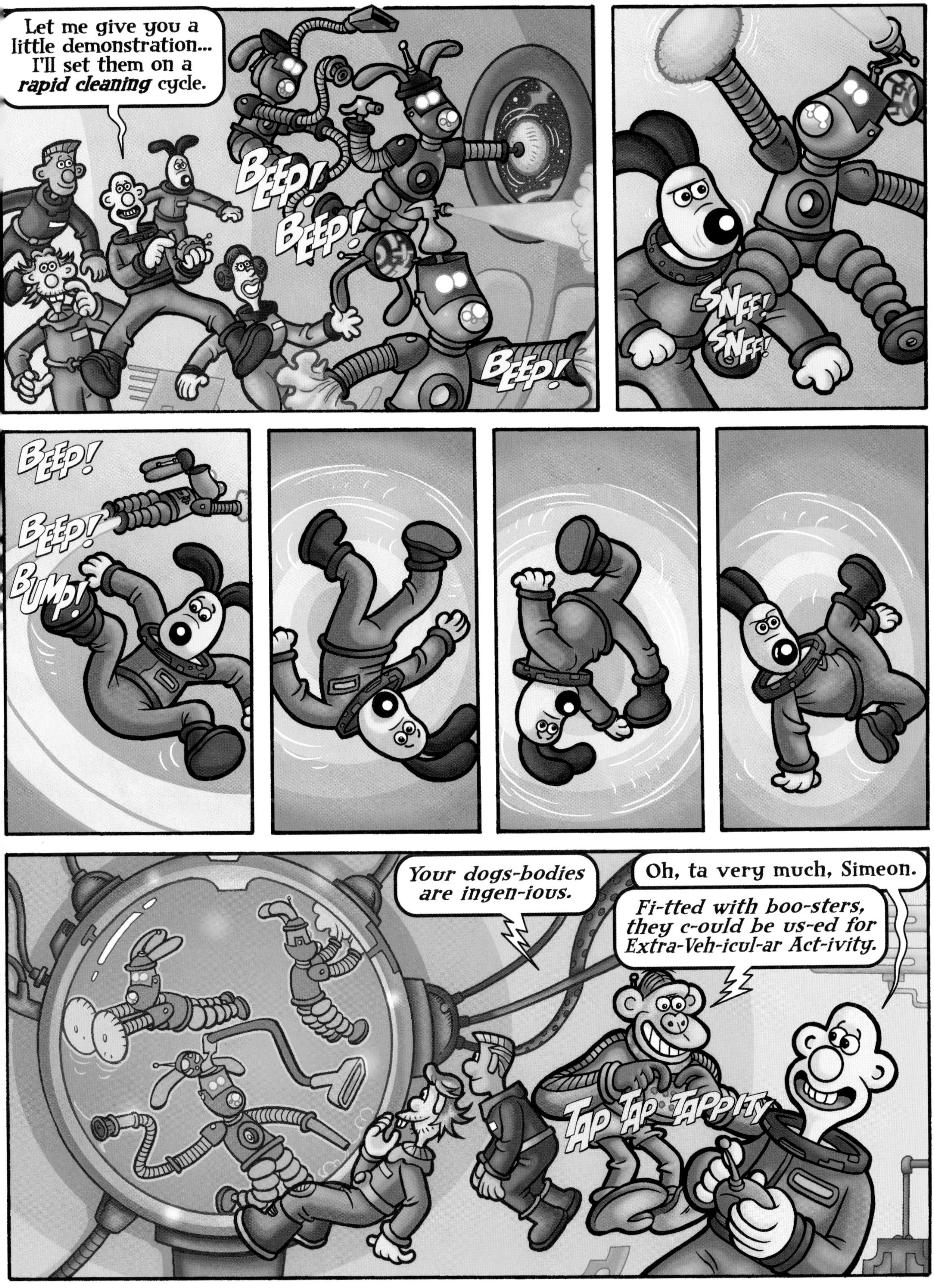
Let me give you a little demonstration... I'll set them on a *rapid cleaning* cycle.
BEEP!
BEEP!
BEEP!
SNFF! SNFF!
BEEP!
BEEP!
BUMP!
Your dogs-bodies are ingen-ious.
Oh, ta very much, Simeon.
Fi-tted with boo-sters, they c-ould be us-ed for Extra-Veh-icul-ar Act-ivity.
TAP TAP TAPPITY

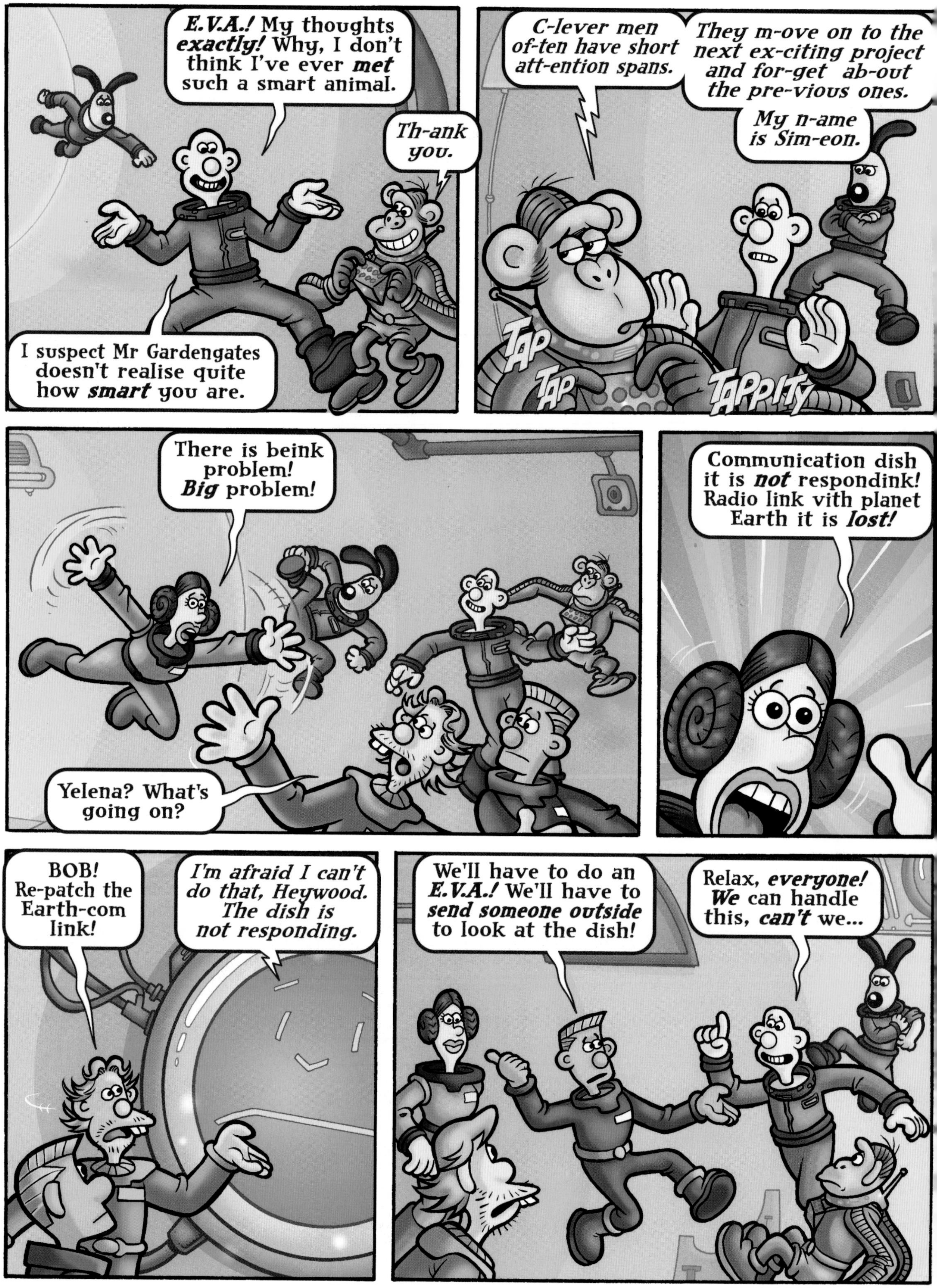
E.V.A.! My thoughts exactly! Why, I don't think I've ever met such a smart animal.
I suspect Mr Gardengates doesn't realise quite how smart you are.
Th-ank you.
C-lever men of-ten have short att-ention spans.
They m-ove on to the next ex-citing project and for-get ab-out the pre-vious ones.
My n-ame is Sim-eon.
TAP
TAP
TAPPITY
There is beink problem! Big problem!
Yelena? What's going on?
Communication dish it is not respondink! Radio link vith planet Earth it is lost!
BOB! Re-patch the Earth-com link!
I'm afraid I can't do that, Heywood. The dish is not responding.
We'll have to do an E.V.A.! We'll have to send someone outside to look at the dish!
Relax, everyone! We can handle this, can't we...

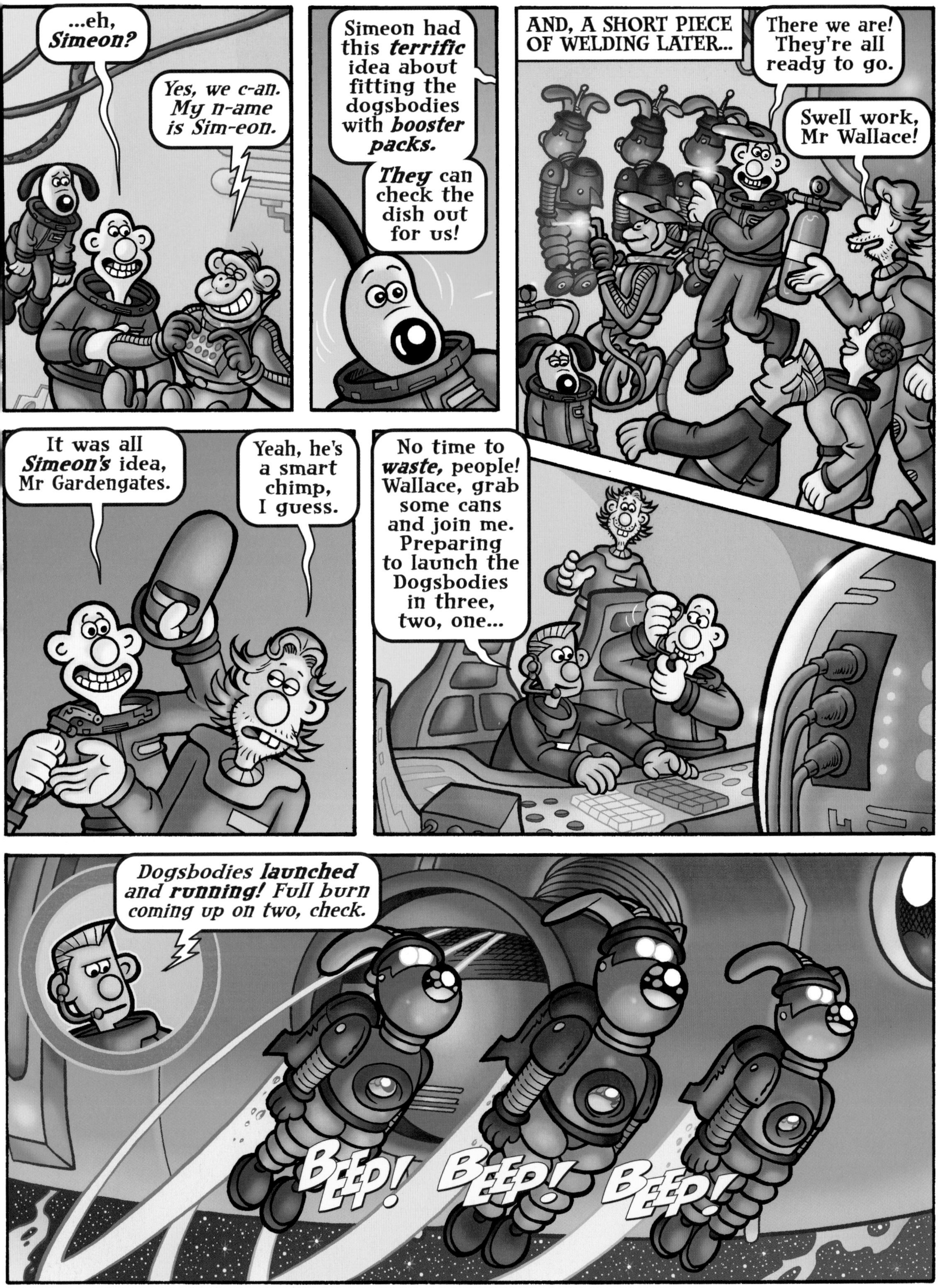

...eh, *Simeon?*
Yes, we c-an. My n-ame is Sim-eon.
Simeon had this ***terrific*** idea about fitting the dogsbodies with ***booster packs.***
They can check the dish out for us!
AND, A SHORT PIECE OF WELDING LATER...
There we are! They're all ready to go.
Swell work, Mr Wallace!
It was all ***Simeon's*** idea, Mr Gardengates.
Yeah, he's a smart chimp, I guess.
No time to ***waste,*** people! Wallace, grab some cans and join me. Preparing to launch the Dogsbodies in three, two, one...
Dogsbodies ***launched*** *and* ***running!*** *Full burn coming up on two, check.*
BEEP! BEEP! BEEP!

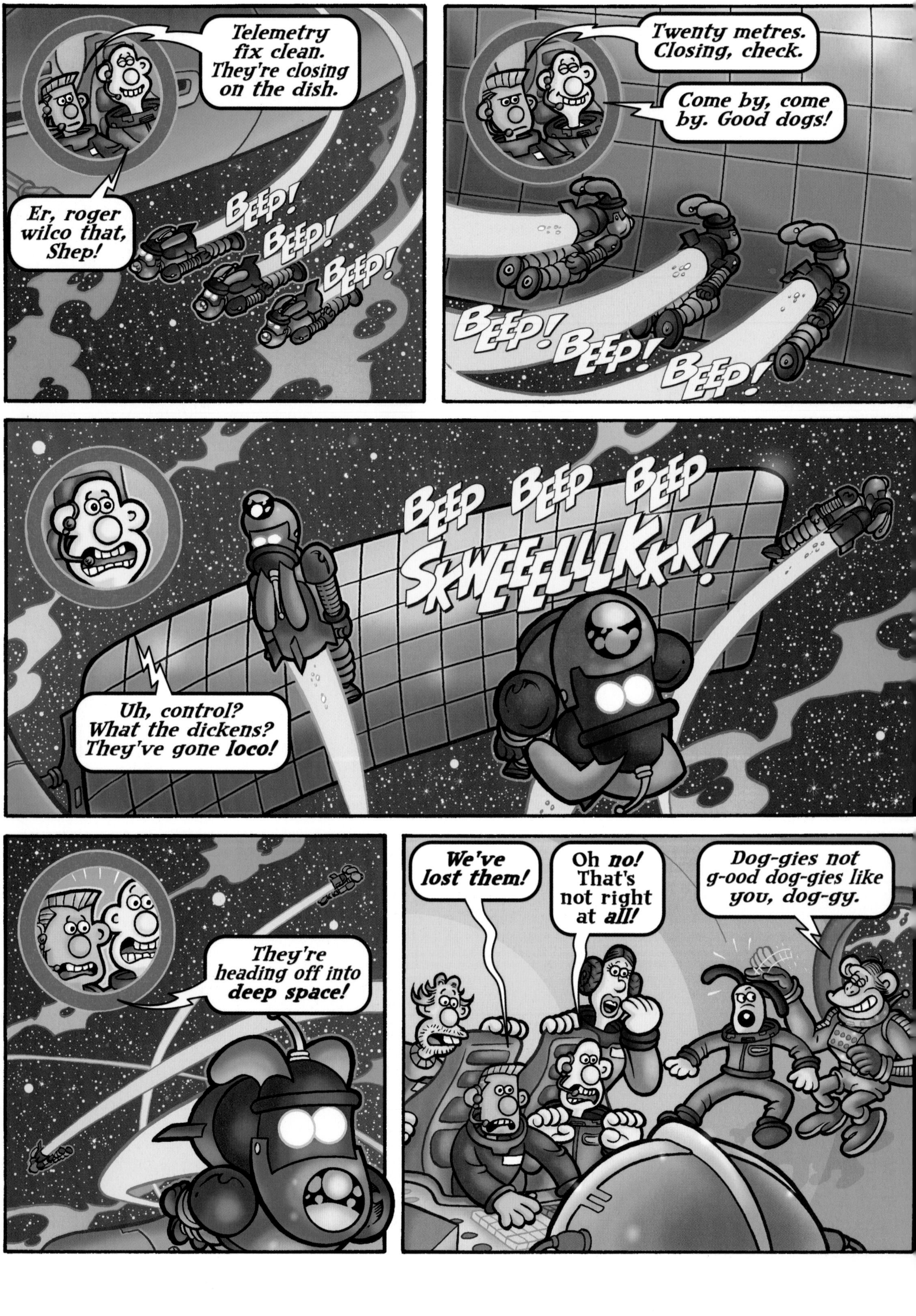
Telemetry fix clean. They're closing on the dish.
Er, roger wilco that, Shep!
BEEP! BEEP! BEEP!
Twenty metres. Closing, check.
Come by, come by. Good dogs!
BEEP! BEEP! BEEP!
BEEP BEEP BEEP
SKWEEEELLLKKK!
Uh, control? What the dickens? They've gone loco!
They're heading off into deep space!
We've lost them!
Oh no! That's not right at all!
Dog-gies not g-ood dog-gies like you, dog-gy.

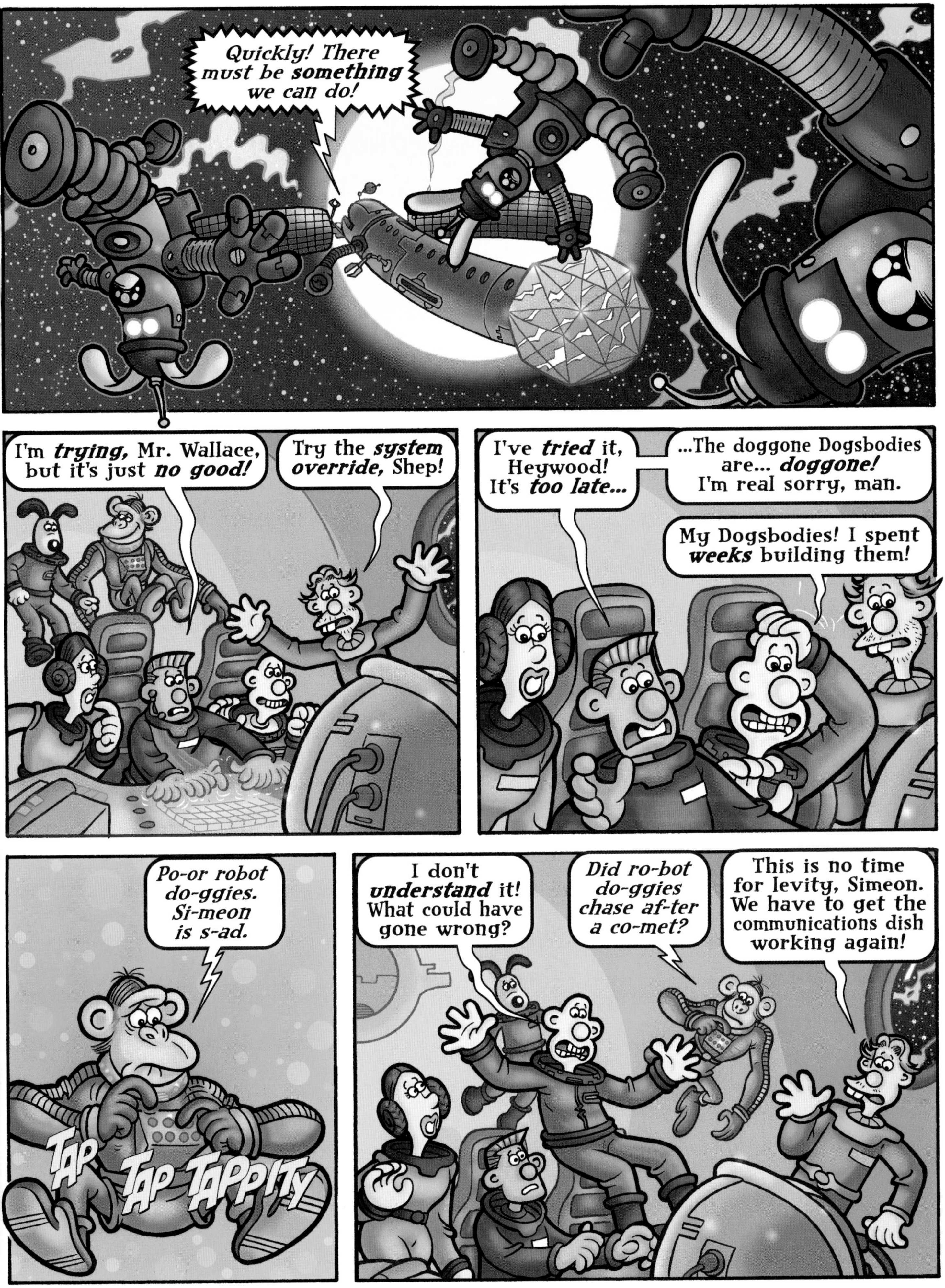
Quickly! There must be something we can do!
I'm trying, Mr. Wallace, but it's just no good!
Try the system override, Shep!
I've tried it, Heywood! It's too late...
...The doggone Dogsbodies are... doggone! I'm real sorry, man.
My Dogsbodies! I spent weeks building them!
Po-or robot do-ggies. Si-meon is s-ad.
TAP TAP TAPPITY
I don't understand it! What could have gone wrong?
Did ro-bot do-ggies chase af-ter a co-met?
This is no time for levity, Simeon. We have to get the communications dish working again!

Well, Mr. Gardengates, the Dogsbodies were *my* responsibility, so there's only *one* person for the job now...

"...Someone who can keep their *feet* on the ground -- even in space...!

MAGNO BOOTS

"...Someone with the *manual dexterity* needed for such a *delicate operation*...

"...Someone with a head for danger and the brains to match!

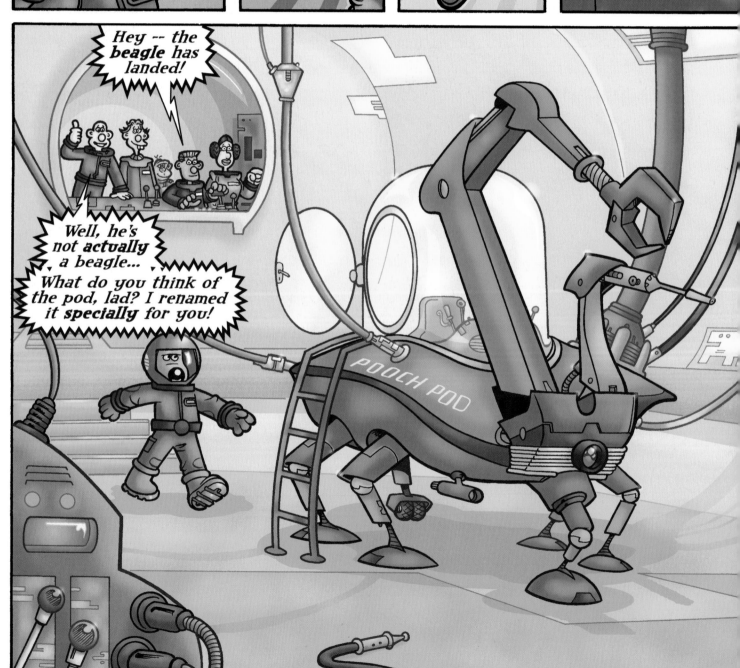

Hey -- the *beagle* has landed!

Well, he's not *actually* a beagle...

What do you think of the pod, lad? I renamed it *specially* for you!

POOCH POD

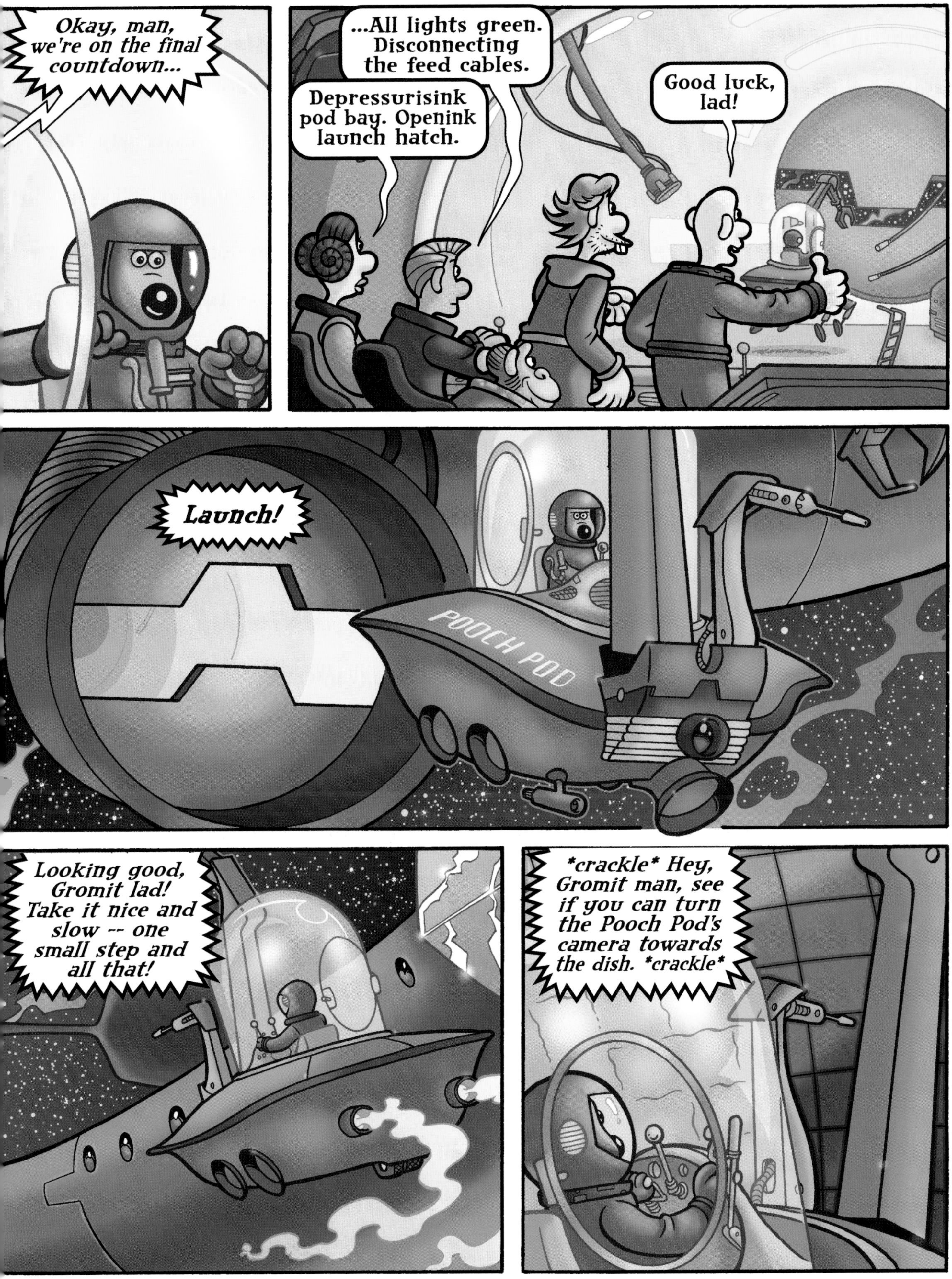
Okay, man, we're on the final countdown...
...All lights green. Disconnecting the feed cables.
Depressurisink pod bay. Openink launch hatch.
Good luck, lad!
Launch!
POOCH POD
Looking good, Gromit lad! Take it nice and slow -- one small step and all that!
crackle Hey, Gromit man, see if you can turn the Pooch Pod's camera towards the dish. *crackle*

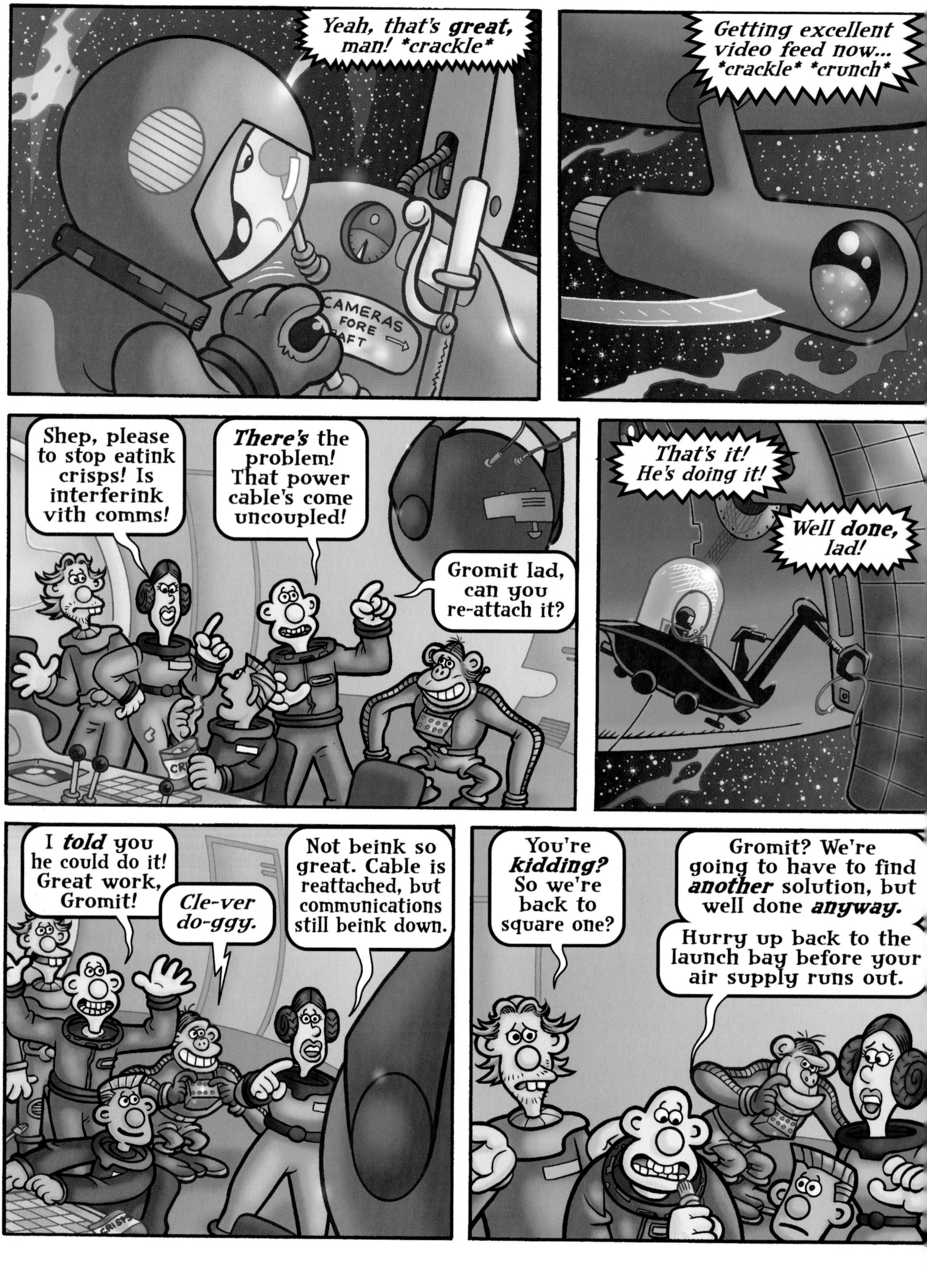
Yeah, that's great, man! *crackle*
CAMERAS FORE AFT
Getting excellent video feed now... *crackle* *crunch*
Shep, please to stop eatink crisps! Is interferink vith comms!
There's the problem! That power cable's come uncoupled!
Gromit lad, can you re-attach it?
That's it! He's doing it!
Well done, lad!
I told you he could do it! Great work, Gromit!
Cle-ver do-ggy.
Not beink so great. Cable is reattached, but communications still beink down.
You're kidding? So we're back to square one?
Gromit? We're going to have to find another solution, but well done anyway.
Hurry up back to the launch bay before your air supply runs out.

SOON...

Hey, the pod bay hatch is **closed**! He can't get in!

Well, open it, then!

The controls are out!

THE CURRY HOUSE TAKE A WAY

BURGER QUEEN

CHOW CHINESE CUISINE

NO JUNK MAIL

ITALIAN PIZZA THE BEST

BOB! Override! Open the pod bay doors!

I'm *sorry*, Heywood. I'm afraid I can't do that.

What? **Why?**

...

I'm busy.

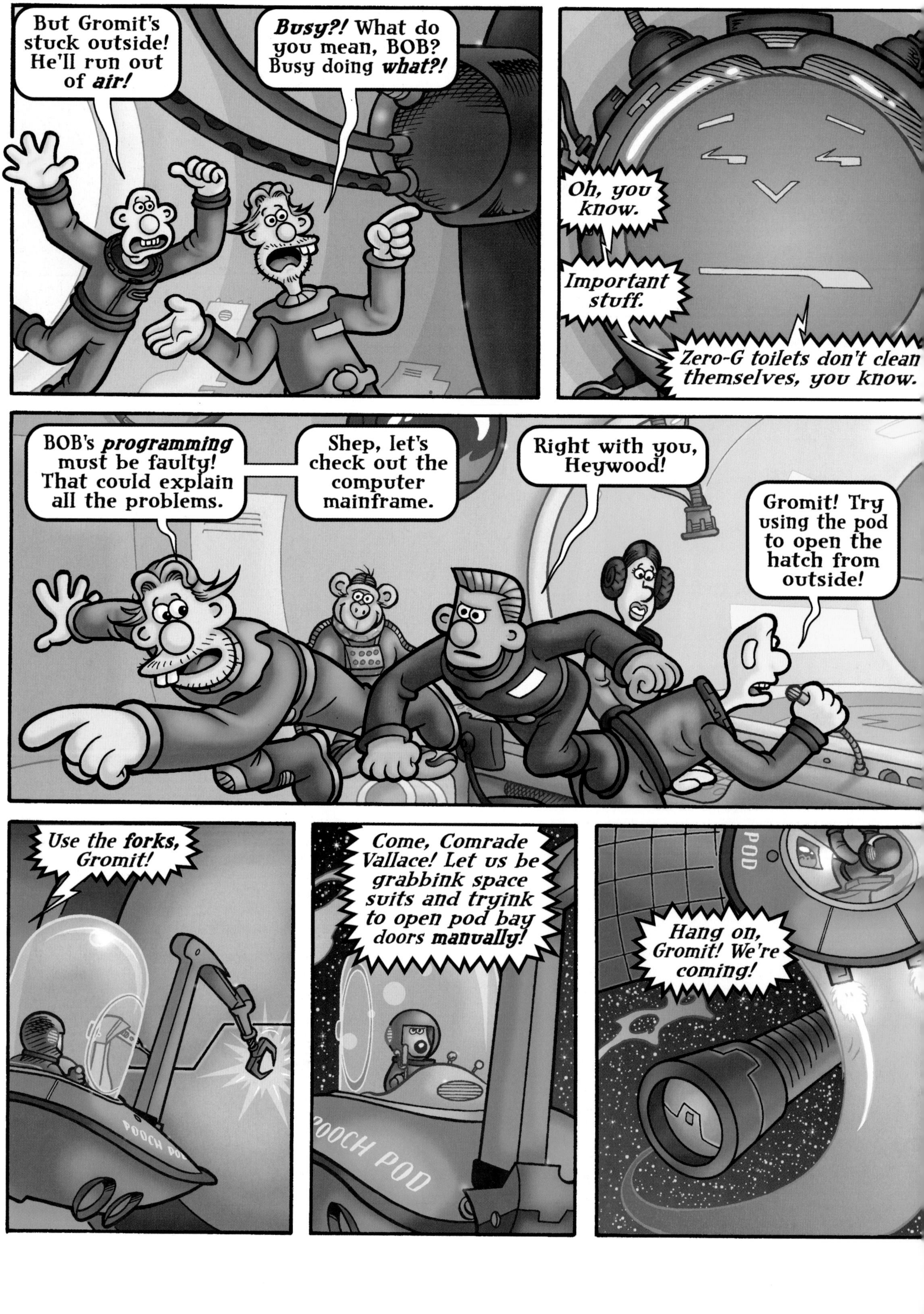

But Gromit's stuck outside! He'll run out of *air!*
Busy?! What do you mean, BOB? Busy doing *what?!*
Oh, you know.
Important stuff.
Zero-G toilets don't clean themselves, you know.
BOB's *programming* must be faulty! That could explain all the problems.
Shep, let's check out the computer mainframe.
Right with you, Heywood!
Gromit! Try using the pod to open the hatch from outside!
Use the **forks,** Gromit!
POOCH POD
Come, Comrade Vallace! Let us be grabbink space suits and tryink to open pod bay doors **manually!**
POOCH POD
POD
Hang on, Gromit! We're coming!

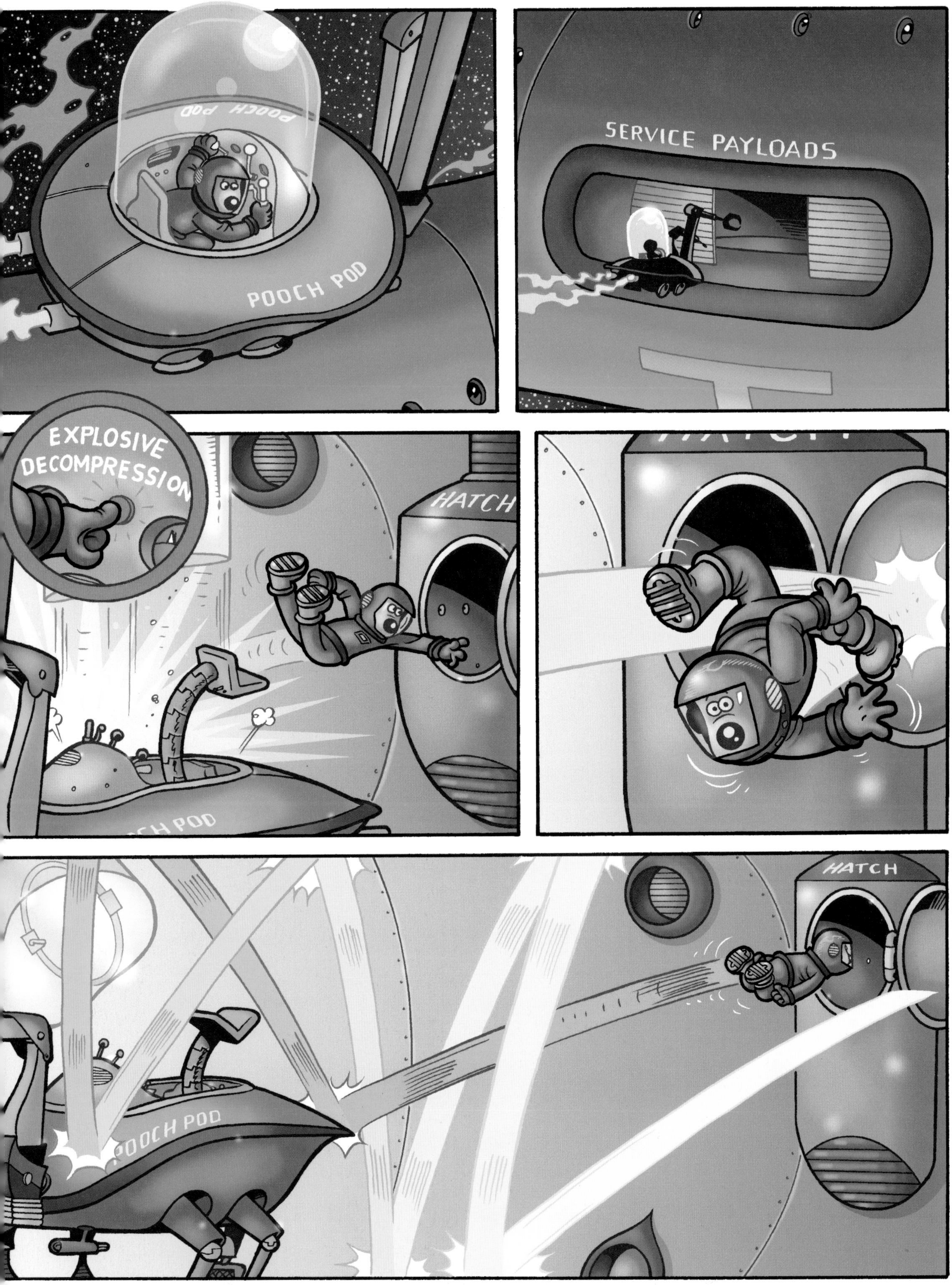
POOCH POD
SERVICE PAYLOADS
EXPLOSIVE DECOMPRESSION
HATCH
HATCH
POOCH POD

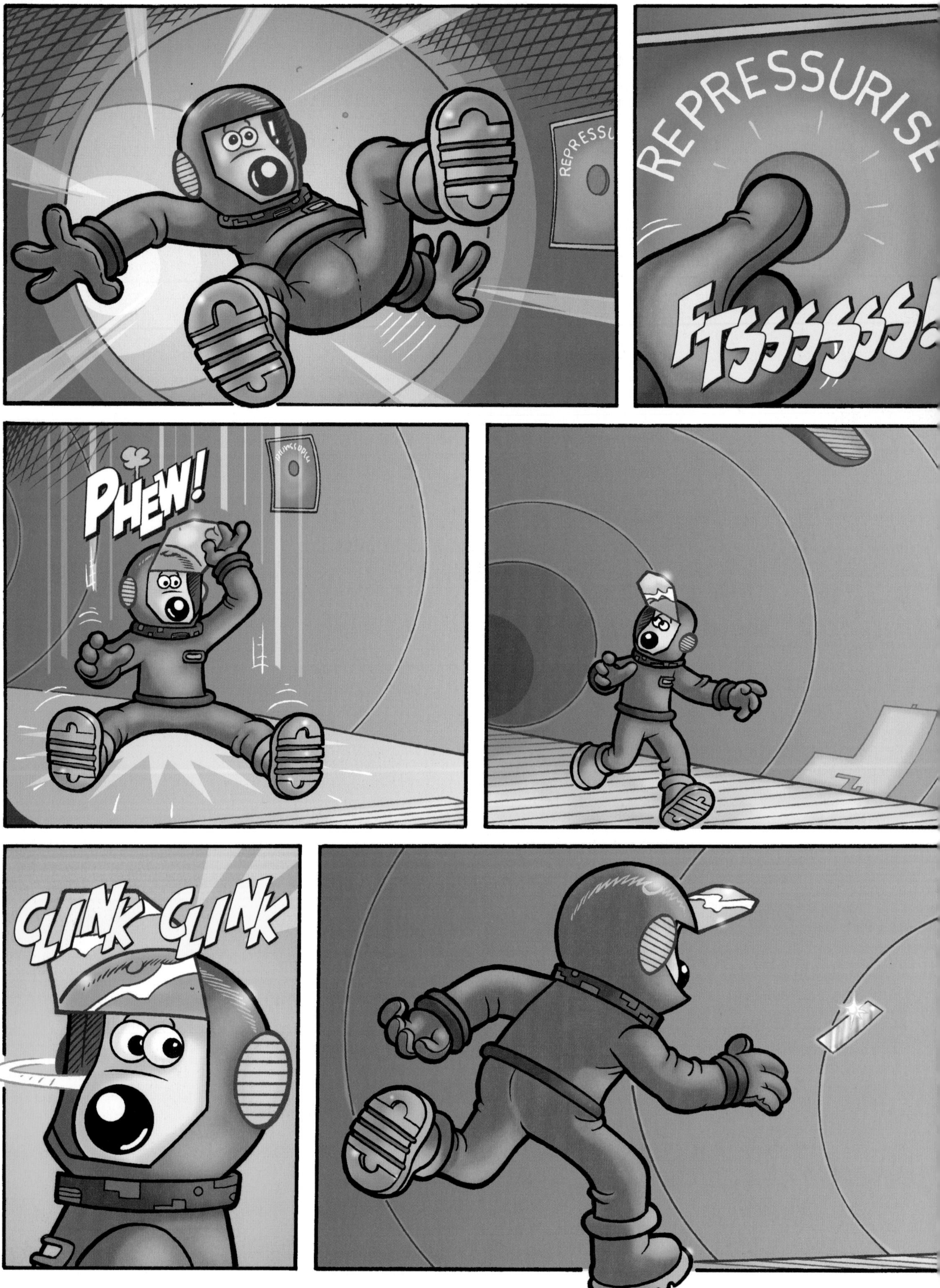

REPRESSURISE
FTSSSSSSS!
PHEW!
CLINK CLINK

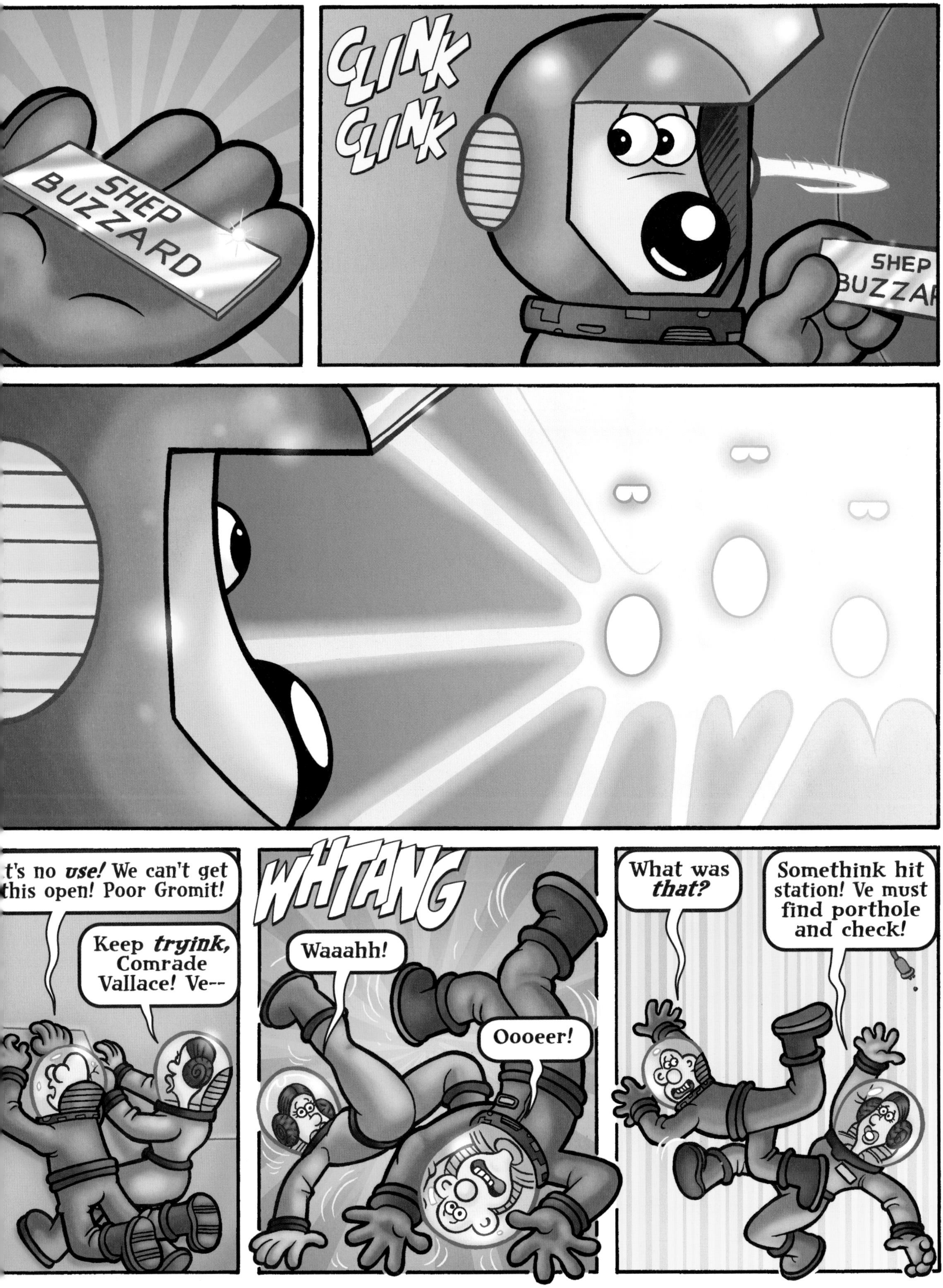
SHEP
BUZZARD
CLINK
CLINK
SHEP
BUZZAR
t's no use! We can't get this open! Poor Gromit!
Keep tryink, Comrade Vallace! Ve--
WHTANG
Waaahh!
Oooeer!
What was that?
Somethink hit station! Ve must find porthole and check!

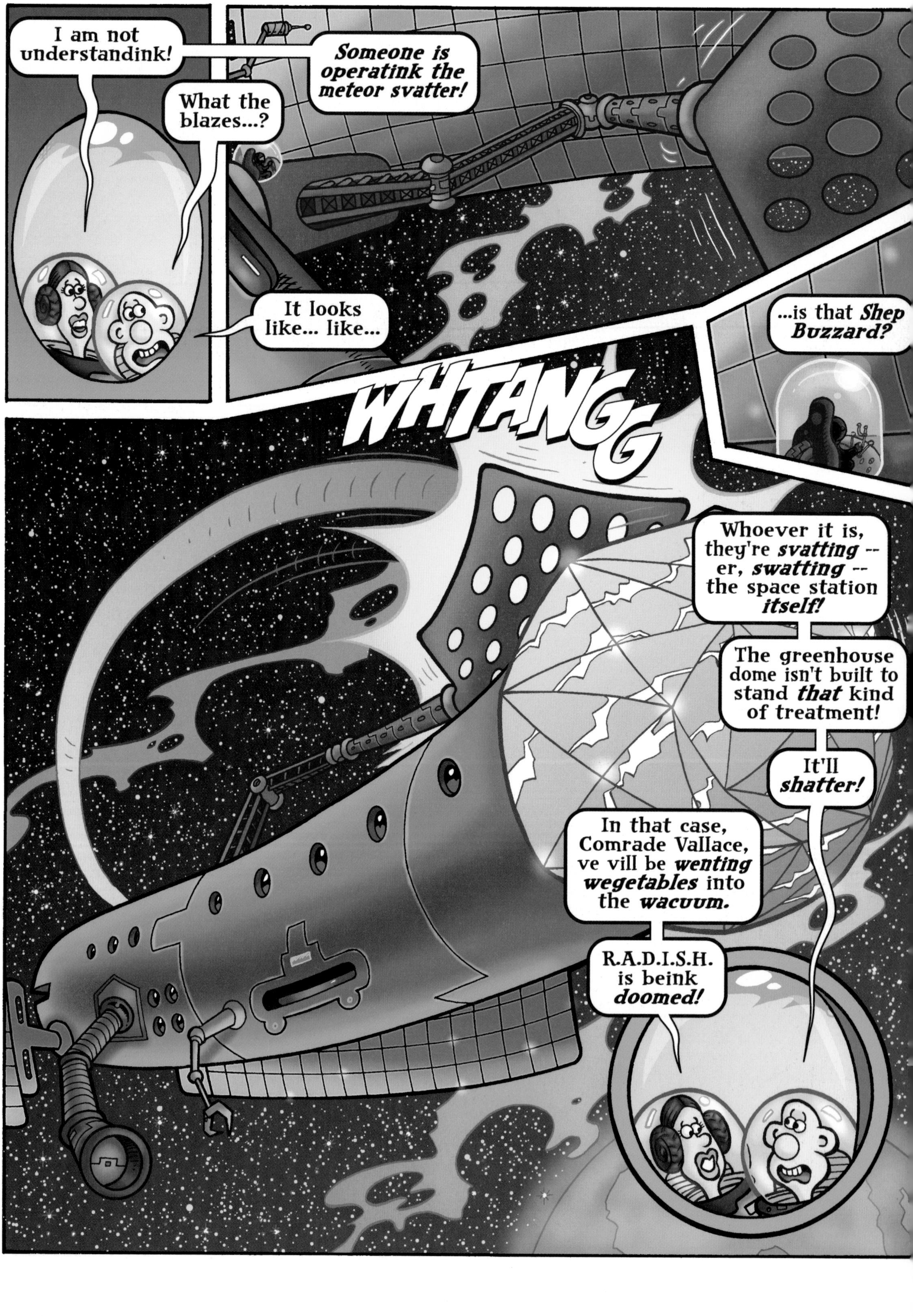
I am not understandink!
Someone is operatink the meteor svatter!
What the blazes...?
It looks like... like...
...is that Shep Buzzard?
WHTANGG
Whoever it is, they're svatting -- er, swatting -- the space station itself!
The greenhouse dome isn't built to stand that kind of treatment!
It'll shatter!
In that case, Comrade Vallace, ve vill be wenting wegetables into the wacuum.
R.A.D.I.S.H. is beink doomed!

BEEP! BEEP! BEEP! BEEP!

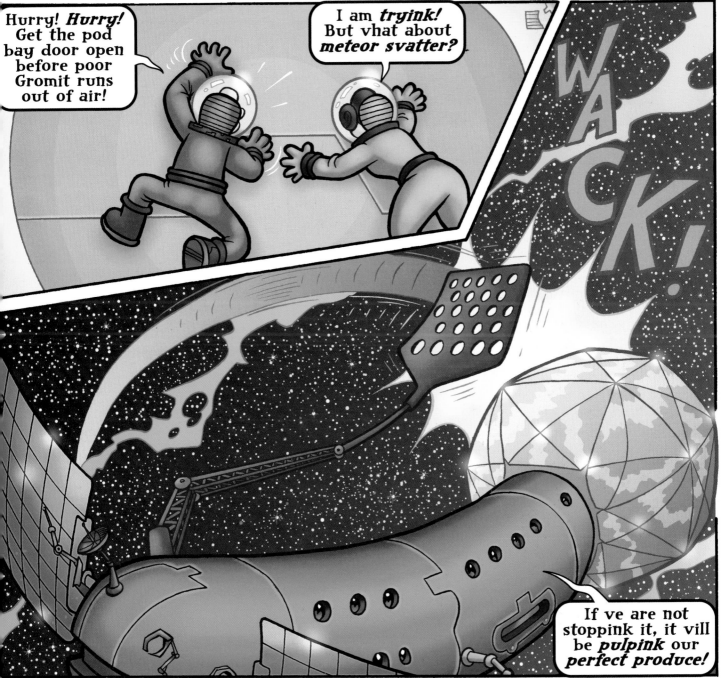

Hurry! *Hurry!* Get the pod bay door open before poor Gromit runs out of air!

I am *tryink!* But vhat about *meteor svatter?*

WACK!

If ve are not *stoppink* it, it vill be *pulpink* our *perfect produce!*

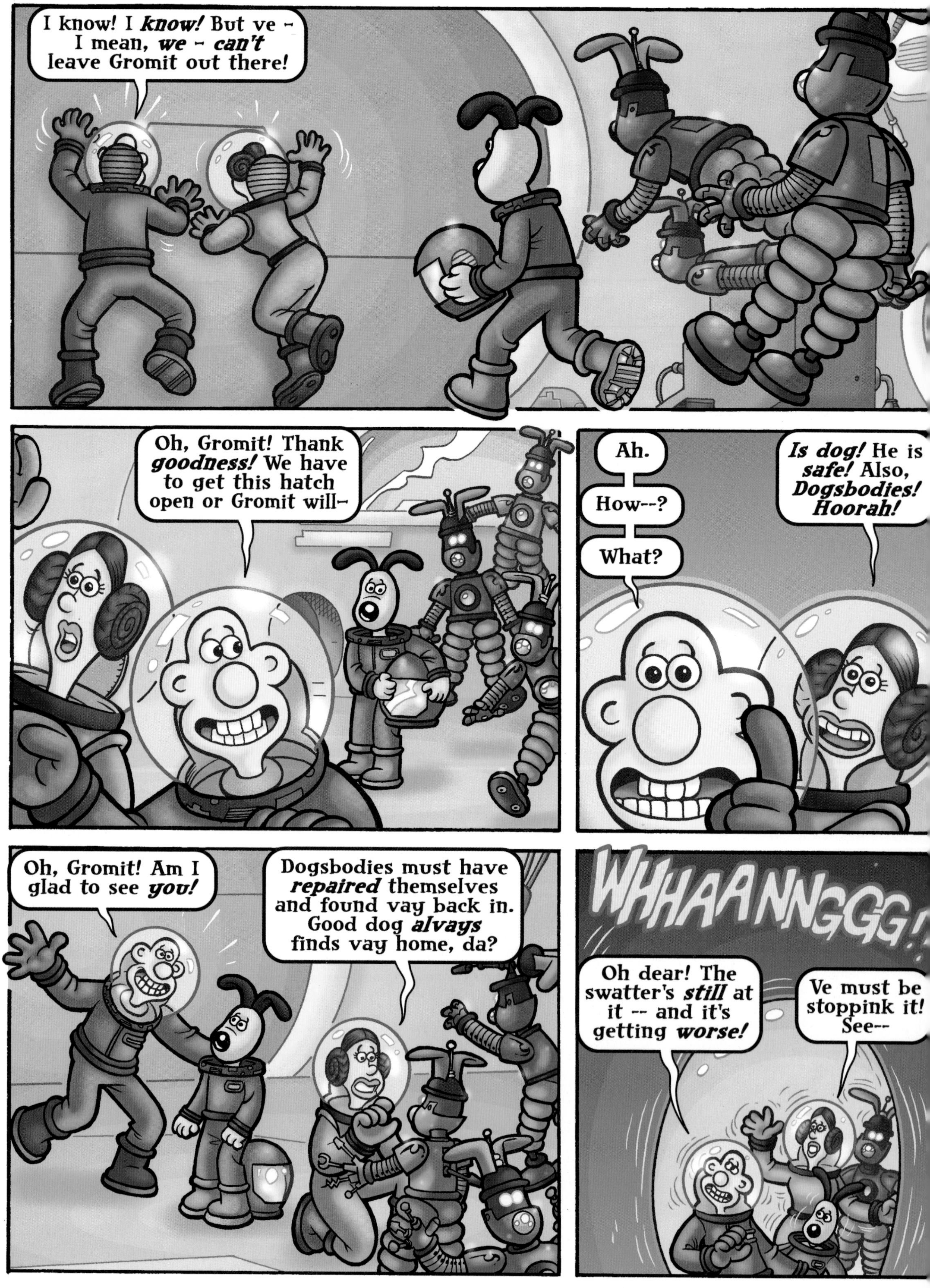
I know! I *know!* But ve – I mean, *we* – *can't* leave Gromit out there!
Oh, Gromit! Thank *goodness!* We have to get this hatch open or Gromit will–
Ah.
How--?
What?
Is dog! He is *safe!* Also, *Dogsbodies! Hoorah!*
Oh, Gromit! Am I glad to see *you!*
Dogsbodies must have *repaired* themselves and found vay back in. Good dog *alvays* finds vay home, da?
WHHAANNGGG!!
Oh dear! The swatter's *still* at it -- and it's getting *worse!*
Ve must be stoppink it! See--

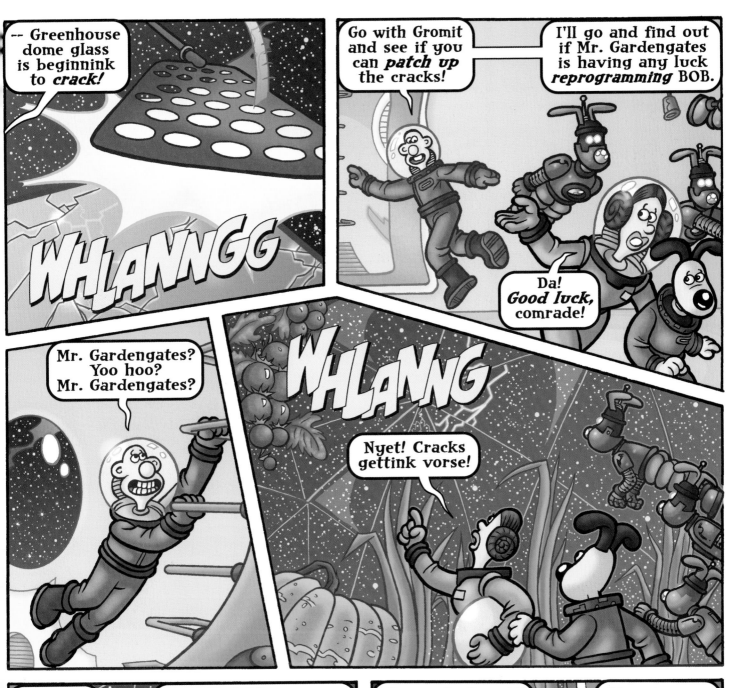

-- Greenhouse dome glass is beginnink to *crack!*

WHLANNGG

Go with Gromit and see if you can *patch up* the cracks!

I'll go and find out if Mr. Gardengates is having any luck *reprogramming* BOB.

Da! *Good luck,* comrade!

Mr. Gardengates? Yoo hoo? Mr. Gardengates?

WHLANNG

Nyet! Cracks gettink vorse!

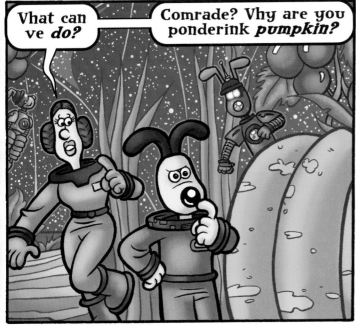

Vhat can ve *do?*

Comrade? Vhy are you ponderink *pumpkin?*

Comrade Gromit! Is no time for playink vith food!

Also, is *wery* bad manners!

SHLUP

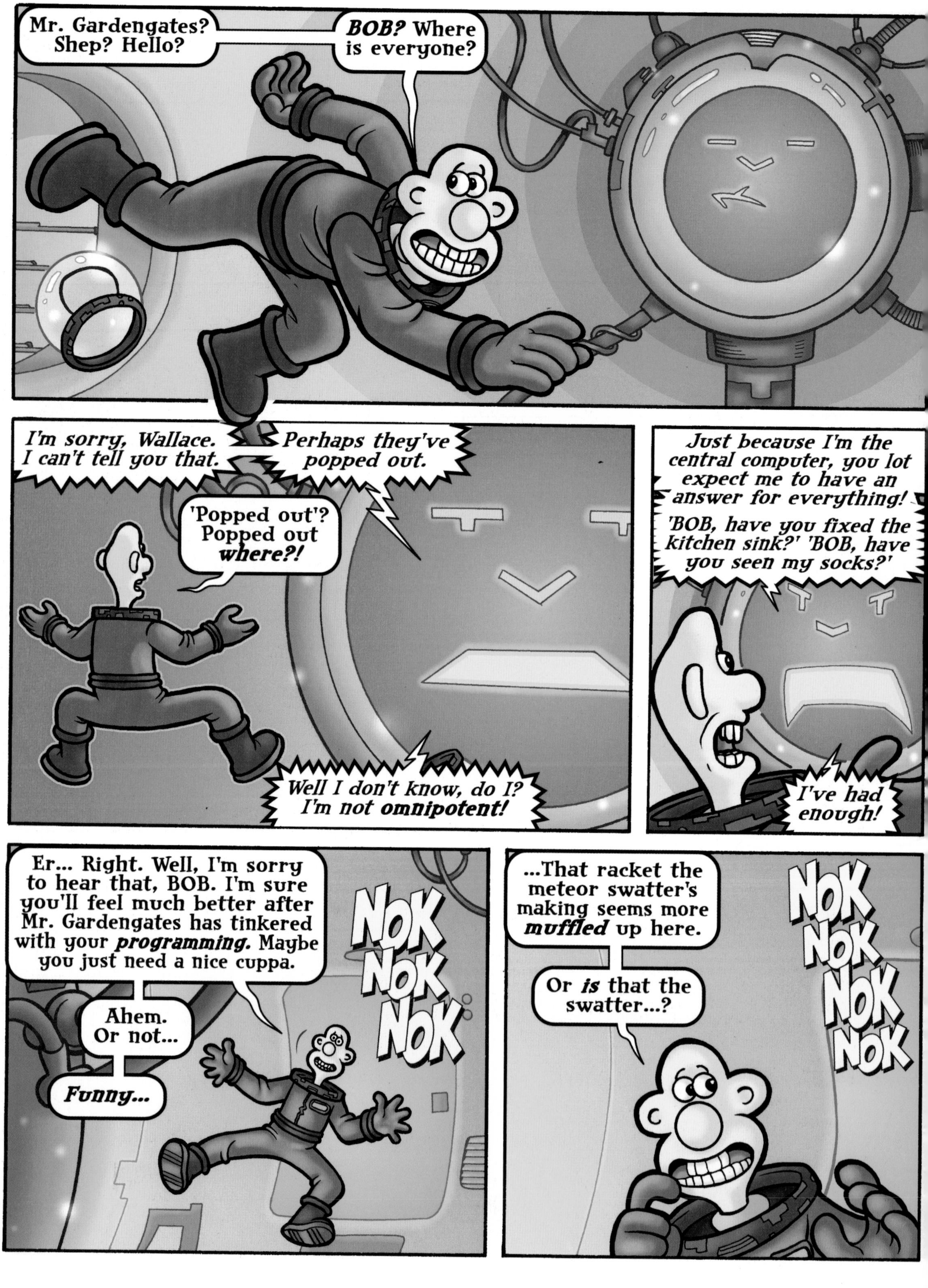
Mr. Gardengates? Shep? Hello?
BOB? Where is everyone?
I'm sorry, Wallace. I can't tell you that.
Perhaps they've popped out.
'Popped out'? Popped out where?!
Well I don't know, do I? I'm not omnipotent!
Just because I'm the central computer, you lot expect me to have an answer for everything!
'BOB, have you fixed the kitchen sink?' 'BOB, have you seen my socks?'
I've had enough!
Er... Right. Well, I'm sorry to hear that, BOB. I'm sure you'll feel much better after Mr. Gardengates has tinkered with your programming. Maybe you just need a nice cuppa.
Ahem. Or not...
Funny...
NOK NOK NOK
...That racket the meteor swatter's making seems more muffled up here.
Or is that the swatter...?
NOK NOK NOK NOK

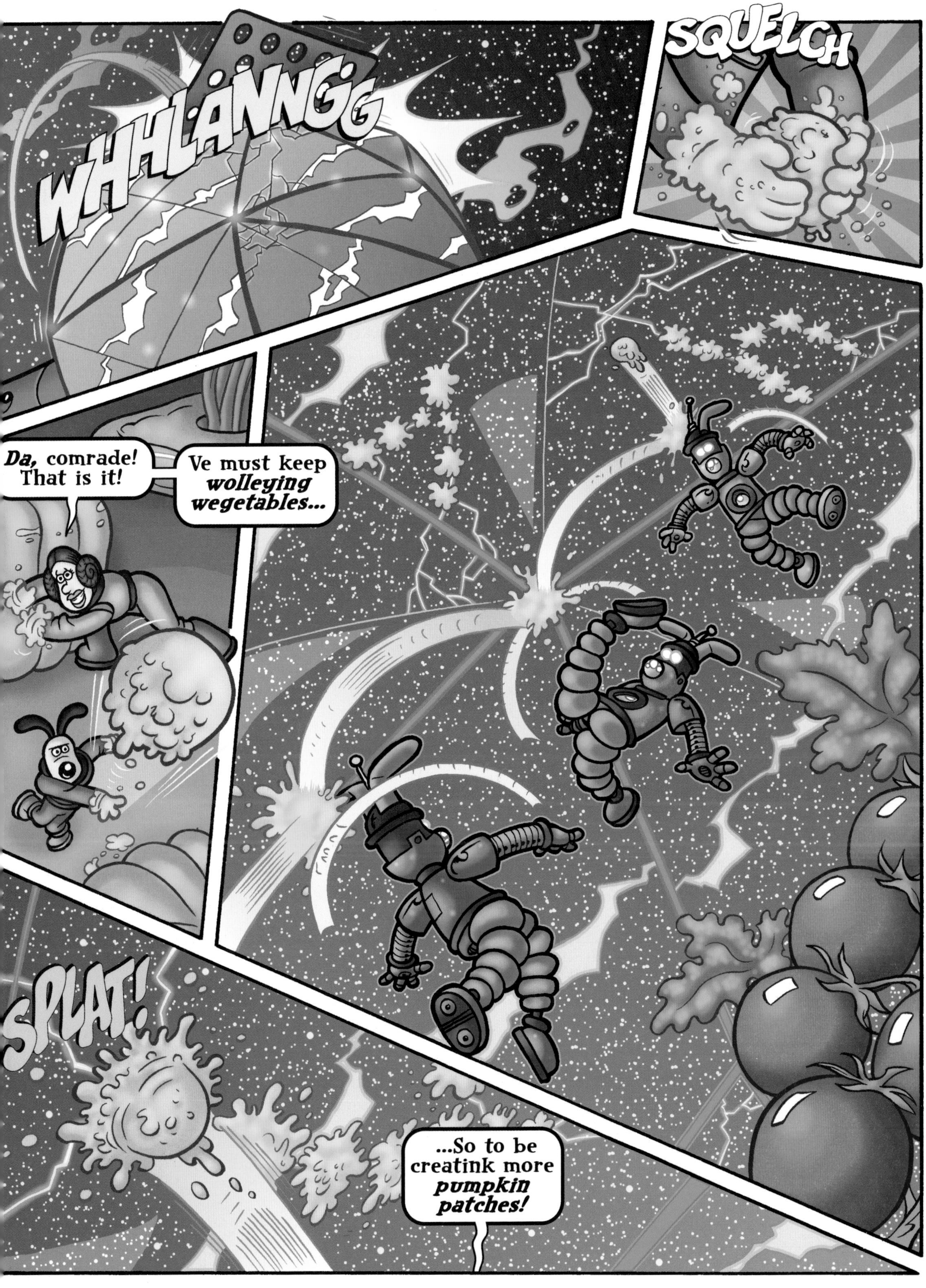
WHHLANNGG
SQUELCH
Da, comrade! That is it!
Ve must keep wolleying wegetables...
SPLAT!
...So to be creatink more pumpkin patches!

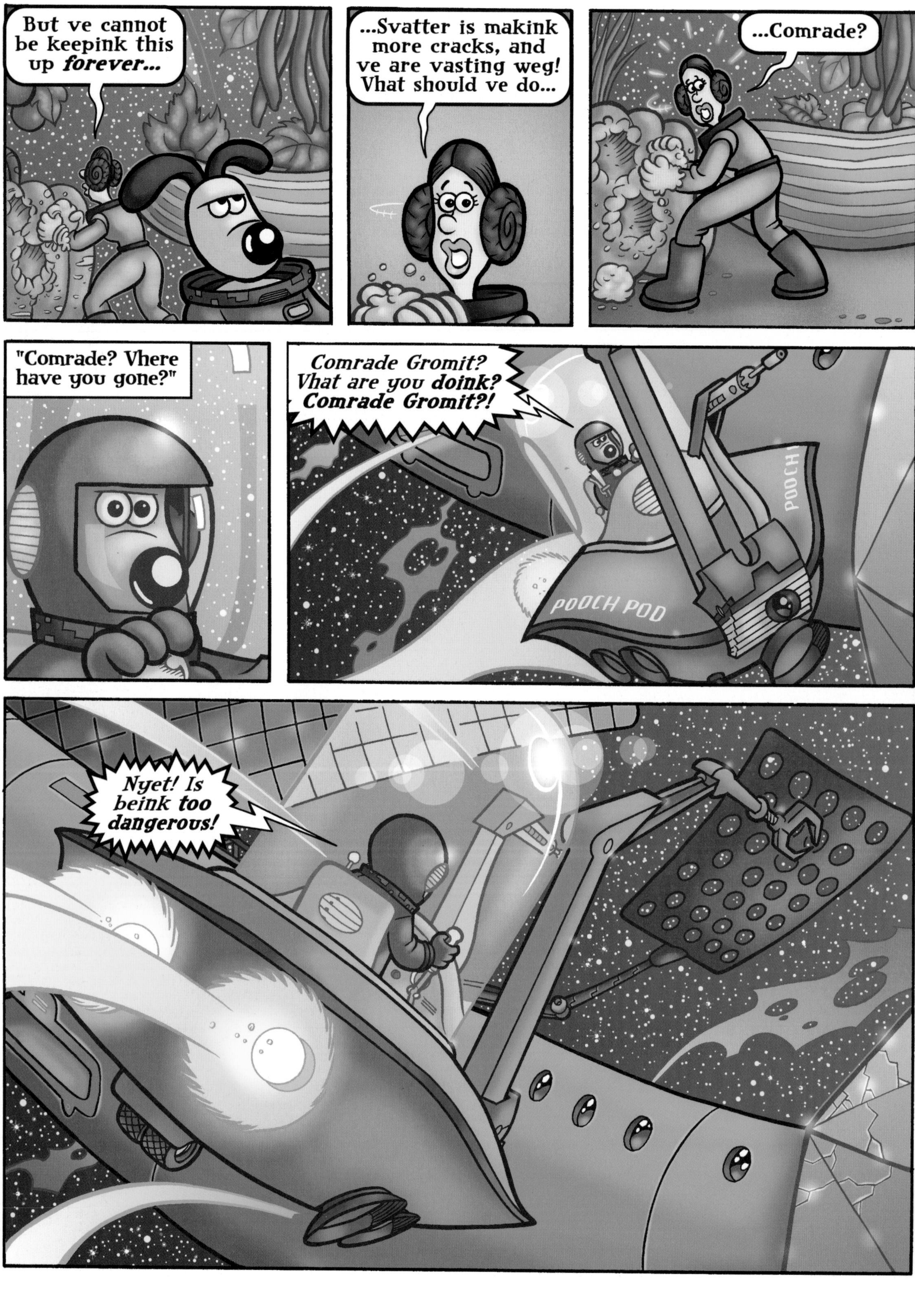

But ve cannot be keepink this up *forever...*
...Svatter is makink more cracks, and ve are vasting weg! Vhat should ve do...
...Comrade?
"Comrade? Vhere have you gone?"
Comrade Gromit? Vhat are you ***doink?*** ***Comrade Gromit?!***
POOCH POD
Nyet! Is beink ***too dangerous!***

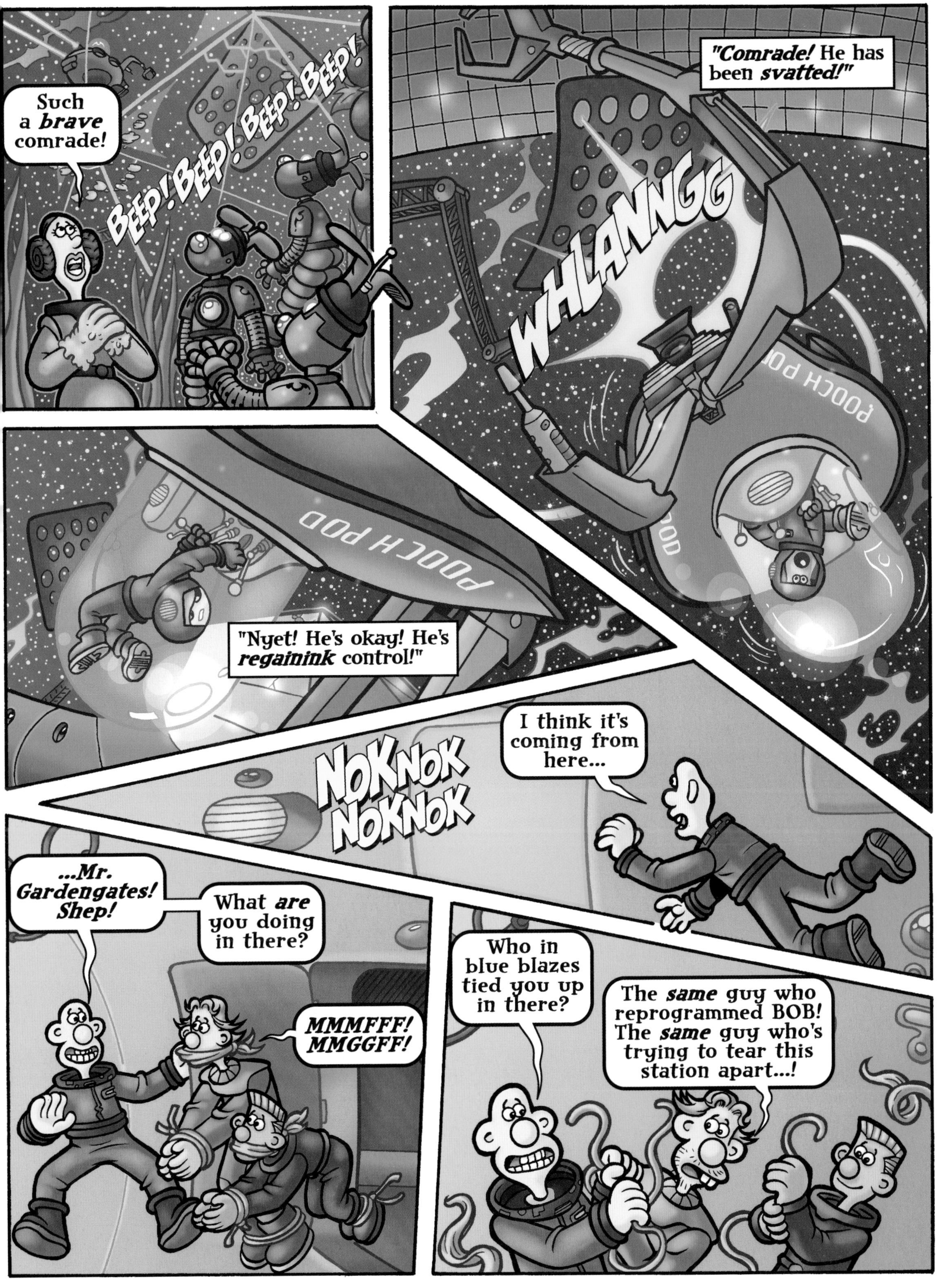
Such a brave comrade!
BEEP! BEEP! BEEP! BEEP! BEEP!
"Comrade! He has been svatted!"
WHLANNGG
POOCH POD
"Nyet! He's okay! He's regainink control!"
I think it's coming from here...
NOKNOK NOKNOK
...Mr. Gardengates! Shep!
What are you doing in there?
MMMFFF! MMGGFF!
Who in blue blazes tied you up in there?
The same guy who reprogrammed BOB! The same guy who's trying to tear this station apart...!

"Simeon!"

You can't stop me now, "dog-gy"!

One more swat, and you'll be space dust!

TAP TAP TAPP'TY TAP

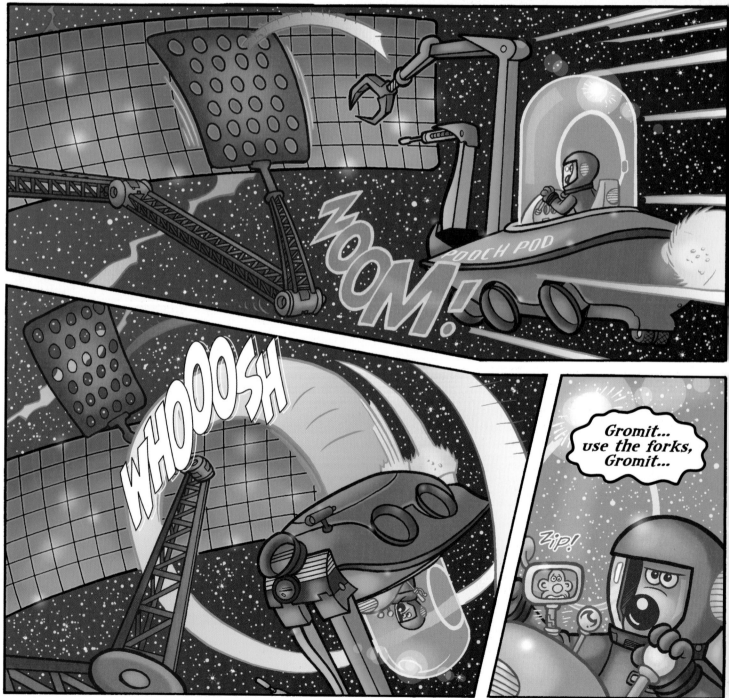

ZOOM!

POOCH POD

WHOOOSH

Gromit... use the forks, Gromit...

Zip!

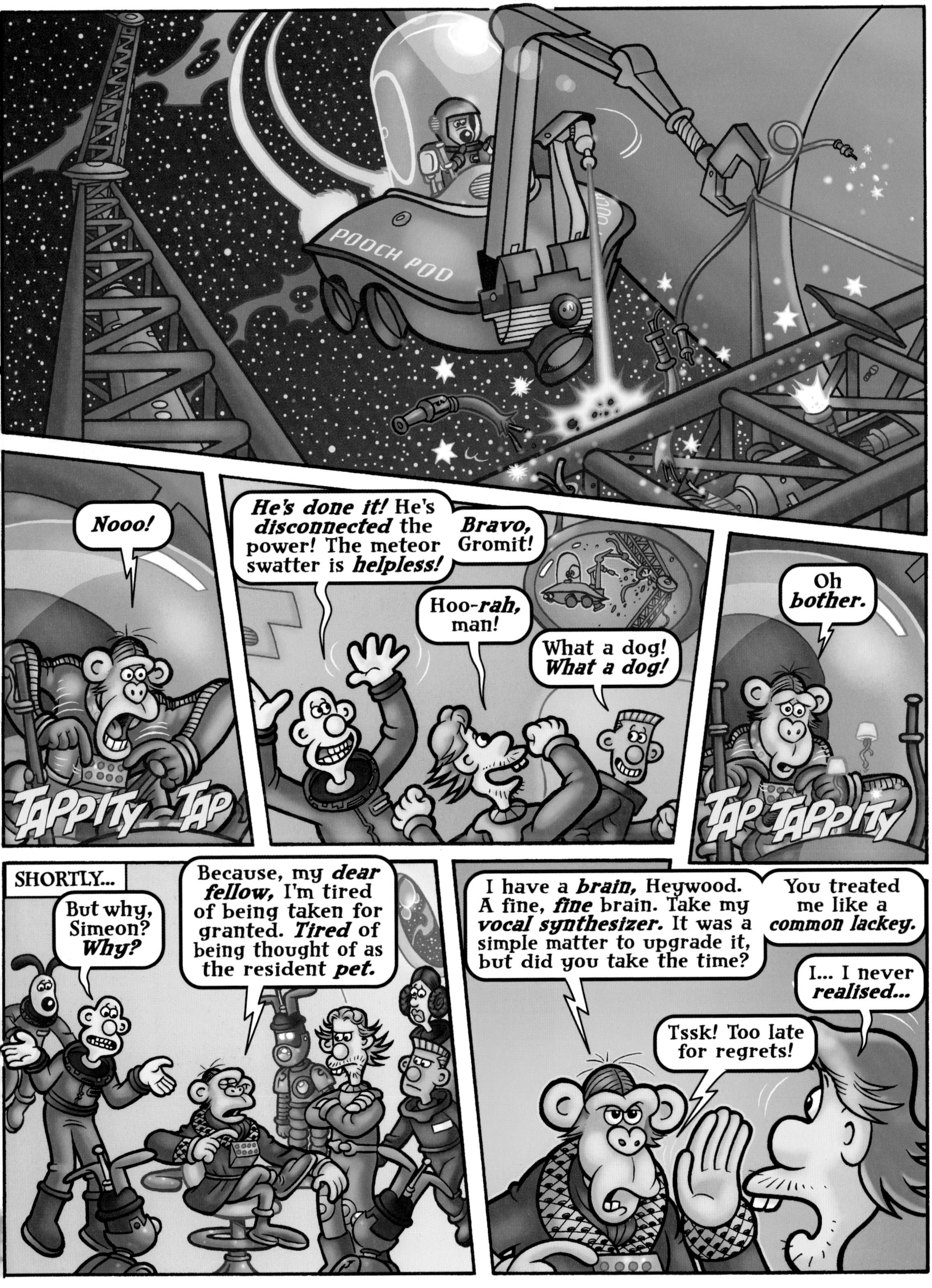

POOCH POD
Nooo!
TAPPITY-TAP
He's done it! He's disconnected the power! The meteor swatter is helpless!
Bravo, Gromit!
Hoo-rah, man!
What a dog! What a dog!
Oh bother.
TAP TAPPITY
SHORTLY...
But why, Simeon? Why?
Because, my dear fellow, I'm tired of being taken for granted. Tired of being thought of as the resident pet.
I have a brain, Heywood. A fine, fine brain. Take my vocal synthesizer. It was a simple matter to upgrade it, but did you take the time?
You treated me like a common lackey.
I... I never realised...
Tssk! Too late for regrets!

But what did you hope to *achieve?*

Surely what we *all* crave... fame, fortune... all the *bananas* I could eat.

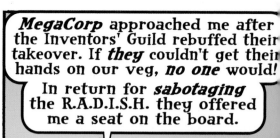

MegaCorp approached me after the Inventors' Guild rebuffed their takeover. If *they* couldn't get their hands on our veg, *no one* would!

In return for *sabotaging* the R.A.D.I.S.H. they offered me a seat on the board.

Well, not so much a *seat* as a new *tyre* to swing on.

MegaCorp? *That* bunch of reprobates again!

I hope they were paying you *well* for your treachery, Simeon.

My dear fellow, they were going to pay me *peanuts.*

Can you *begin* to imagine?

SOME DAYS LATER, BACK ON EARTH...

Oh *look,* lad! It's a postcard from the space station!

GREETINGS FROM SPACE

Seems the *dogsbodies* are working out very nicely. And Heywood says that Simeon's been sent to a *special zoo* to keep him out of mischief.

Come on, lad. Wendolene's *dying* to hear about our extraterrestrial adventures.

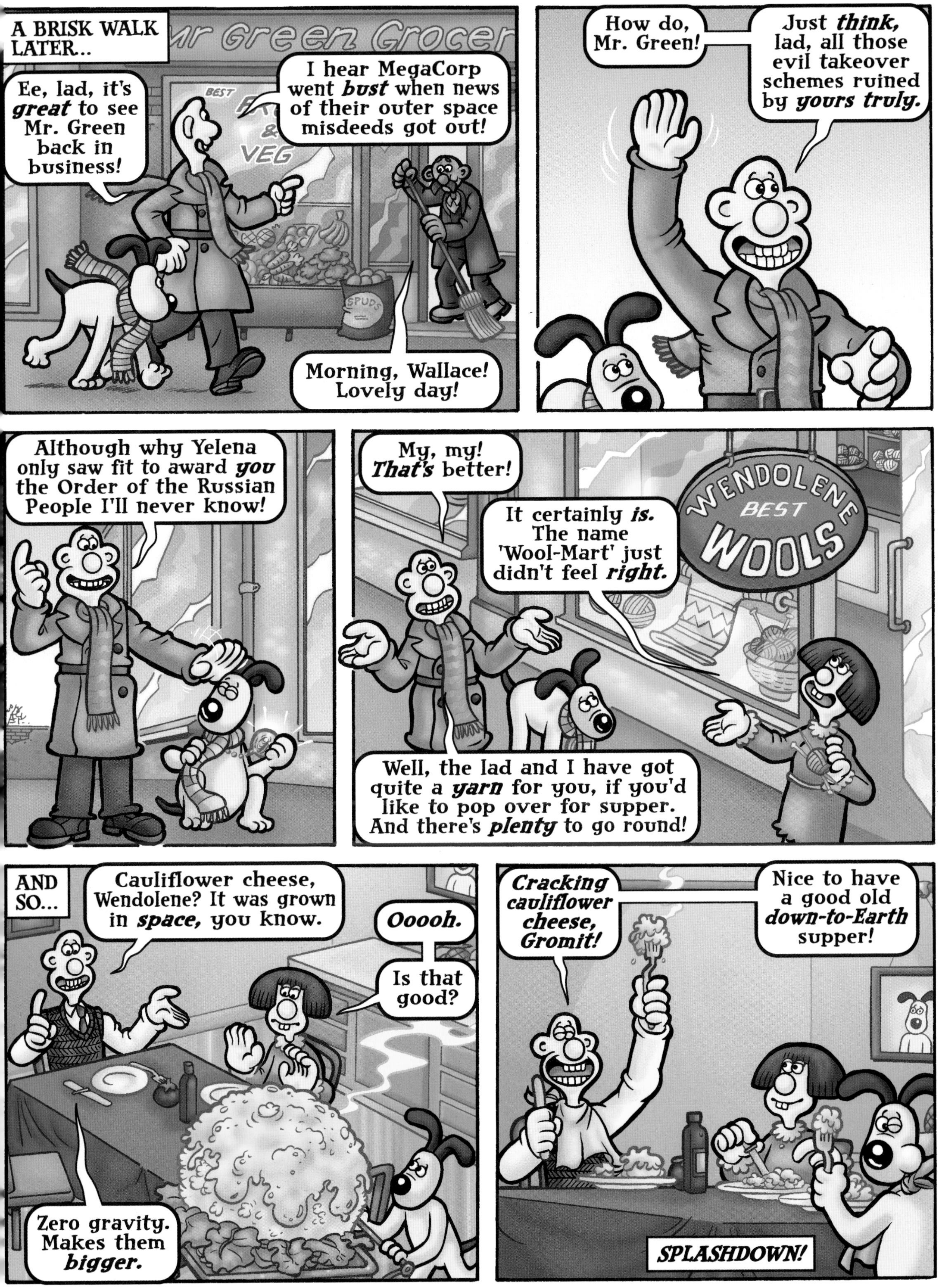
A BRISK WALK LATER...
Mr Green Grocer
Ee, lad, it's great to see Mr. Green back in business!
I hear MegaCorp went bust when news of their outer space misdeeds got out!
Morning, Wallace! Lovely day!
How do, Mr. Green!
Just think, lad, all those evil takeover schemes ruined by yours truly.
Although why Yelena only saw fit to award you the Order of the Russian People I'll never know!
My, my! That's better!
WENDOLENE BEST WOOLS
It certainly is. The name 'Wool-Mart' just didn't feel right.
Well, the lad and I have got quite a yarn for you, if you'd like to pop over for supper. And there's plenty to go round!
AND SO...
Cauliflower cheese, Wendolene? It was grown in space, you know.
Ooooh.
Is that good?
Zero gravity. Makes them bigger.
Cracking cauliflower cheese, Gromit!
Nice to have a good old down-to-Earth supper!
SPLASHDOWN!

CHECK OUT THESE OTHER CRACKING COLLECTIONS FROM TITAN BOOKS!

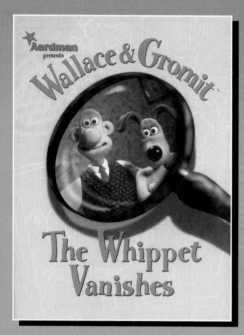

Aardman presents
Wallace & Gromit
The Whippet Vanishes

Wallace & Gromit:
The Whippet Vanishes

Aardman presents
Wallace & Gromit
Catch of the Day

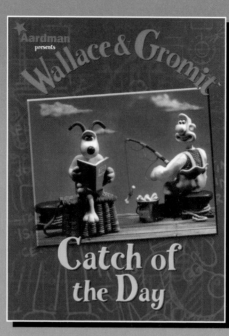

Wallace & Gromit:
Catch of the Day

Aardman presents
Wallace & Gromit
A Pier Too Far

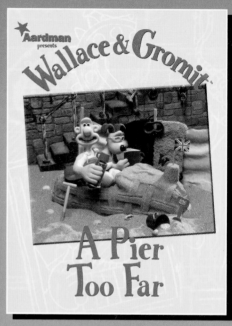

Wallace & Gromit:
A Pier Too Far

Aardman presents
Wallace & Gromit
The Bootiful Game

Wallace & Gromit:
The Bootiful Game

FREE DETECTIVE NOTEBOOK!
Wallace & Gromit
Comic

Wallace & Gromit: The Comic!
Available at all good newsagents

FREE! NOTEPAD & PENCIL!
1st issue
Shaun the Sheep
Comic
BA-A-A-A-ARMY ADVENTURES!
Meet the TV Stars!
Aardman
Bitzer
Naughty Pig
Timmy

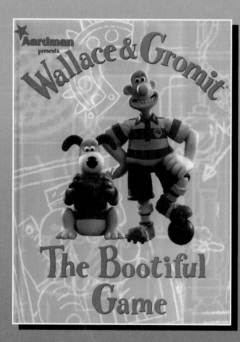

Shaun the Sheep: The Comic!
Available at all good newsagents

www.titanbooks.com

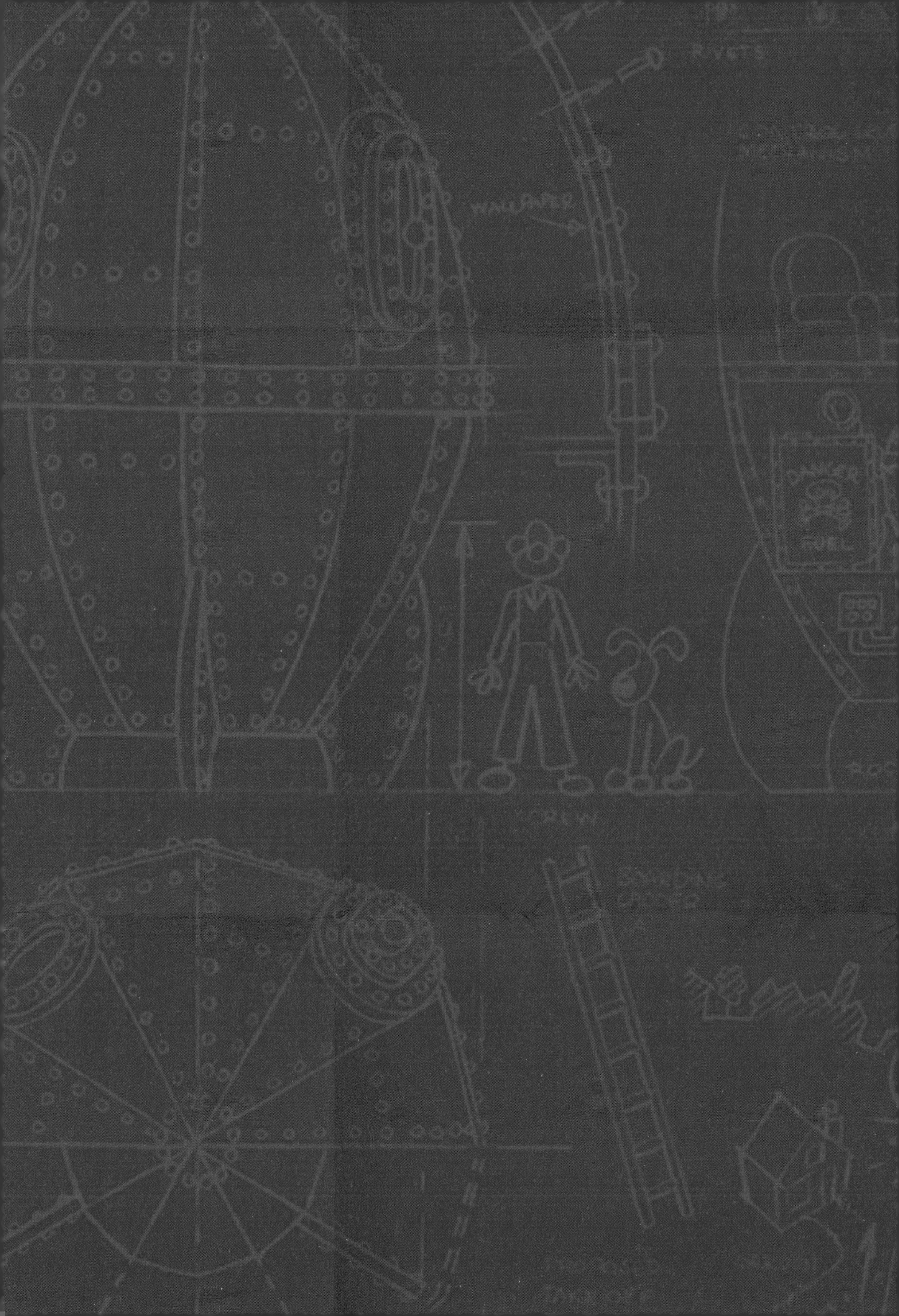
RIVETS
WALLPAPER
FUEL